BUILDING
INNER STRENGTH

This book is edited and designed by the Editorial Committee of *Cultural China* series.

Text by Wang Jueren
Translation by Tony Blishen
Design by Wang Wei
Cover Photo by Getty Images

Copy Editor: Diane Davies
Editor: Wu Yuezhou
Editorial Director: Zhang Yicong

ISBN: 978-1-93836-861-5

Address any comments about *Building Inner Strength* to:

SCPG
401 Broadway, Ste. 1000
New York, NY 10013
USA

or

Shanghai Press and Publishing Development Co., Ltd.
390 Fuzhou Road, Shanghai, China (200001)
Email: sppdbook@163.com

Printed in China by Shanghai Donnelley Printing Co., Ltd.

1   3   5   7   9   10   8   6   4   2

BUILDING INNER STRENGTH

The Chinese Philosophy of Wang Yangming's School of Mind

BY WANG JUEREN
TRANSLATED BY TONY BLISHEN

SCPG

Contents

Take the Road to Spiritual Independence

The world today exists in an era of rapid technological change in which mankind has employed its intelligence and ability to create a material civilization of unprecedented prosperity that strives to make life more convenient, efficient, and comfortable. Regrettably, this highly developed material society does not offer a concomitant meaning to life. A lifestyle that puts consumerism and amusement to the fore does not equate with happiness. This is the inborn illness of modern civilization, its clinical symptoms an all-out search for material prosperity to the progressive detriment of our spiritual life. With our insatiable appetite for more and more possessions, we have allowed our own spiritual self to suffer from an increasingly serious famine. The result is a loss of meaning, an imbalance of life and alienation in human nature that makes the outer world appear ever more dazzlingly attractive, whilst our inner world becomes increasingly depressed, apprehensive, despondent, empty, and bewildered.

Erich Fromm (1900–1980), the German-born Jewish American psychoanalyst and humanist philosopher, believed that in the ancient Greek and Hebrew sources of Western civilization man's lifetime aim was to "seek the perfection of man" but that today contemporary man invariably pursues "the perfection of objects" with the result that man has objectified himself and turned his life into a subsidiary of property. Thus, "to be" is now under the control of "to have" and "existence" is subordinate to "possession."

It is no coincidence that amongst the sources of Chinese culture, particularly in the Confucian thought of pre-Qin philosophy represented by Confucius (551–479 BC) and Mengzi (c. 372–289 BC), "the perfection of man" was the lifetime aim of the Chinese people and, even more, their most lofty spiritual target. One might even say that it was the seat of the meaning of all human life. As the Confucian classic, the *Great Learning*, says: "From emperor to the common people, all should make self-cultivation the foundation of their lives." For the aim of self-cultivation is the perfection of character and self-realization, Fromm's "perfection of man."

Feng Youlan (1895–1990), the modern Chinese Confucian philosopher, expressed the spirit of Chinese philosophy in simple language when he said in *A Short History of Chinese Philosophy*: "There are all kinds and conditions of men. With regard to any one of these kinds, there is the highest form of achievement of which any one kind of man is capable. For instance, there are the men engaged in practical politics. The highest form of achievement in that class of men is that of the great statesman. So also, in the field of art, the highest form of achievement of which artists are capable is that of the great artist. Although there are these different classes of men, yet all of them are men. What is the highest form of achievement of which a man as a man is capable? According to the Chinese philosophers, it is nothing less than being a sage."

A sage is someone whose character is at the zenith of perfection and whose spirit is free and independent through and through. Confucius once described his own experience of a life of study from, "at fifteen I had the will to study perfection of character" to, "at seventy all that I desired fell within prescribed limits." Clearly, it is this state that is one of absolute spiritual independence.

As the Confucians saw it, the search for the meaning of life and the ability to live the kind of worthwhile life described above were, purely on a material plane, unachievable: effort was also required on a spiritual plane. Put another way, to be like Confucius, the goal of ultimate spiritual independence must be achieved through the perfection of character. It is only in this way that the meaning and value of life can grow and the hope for true joy, happiness, and success can be realized.

However, is it possible that for ordinary people like us, this kind of Chinese philosophical life is beyond our reach?

This is a superfluous anxiety. Confucius said: "Is *Ren* (humanity) far? If I desire it, it will arrive." Mengzi said: "Man may be as Yao and Shun (mythological sage kings)."

Ren is the highest moral quality of Confucianism and Yao and Shun its most revered examples of integrity of character. Confucius and Mengzi were certain that everybody could possess the virtue of *Ren* and become a sage because they believed that each and every one of us possessed the potential.

Then, what should we do to fully realize this potential? What is there, really, that can allow us to find the meaning of life and live a worthwhile life?

Wang Yangming (1472–1529), the great Ming dynasty (1368–1644) Confucian scholar and direct transmitter of the spirit of Confucius and Mengzi, had an extremely concise answer: the exercise of conscience.

In the language of Wang Yangming's School of Mind, there are two levels of meaning to the word "conscience": a moral awareness common to all life and innate in man and, secondly, a universal source, intrinsic to man, that transcends all living things.

In this context, "universe" is not the physical universe of science but the philosophical universe of the spirit. The exploration of the physical universe has its origins in the inquisitive tendencies of man but his questions about the spiritual universe derive from concerns that are deeply rooted in his nature. As we become man from birth, the life that we possess is in the end limited, temporary, and relative. Yet, at the same time, in the depths of the soul, mankind is always yearning and seeking for the unlimited, the perpetual, and the absolute. Consequently, the great majority of the world's religions and philosophies are built upon the original substance of the spiritual universe of the individual. This applies to the God of Christianity, the Tathata of Buddhism, and the Allah of Islam; to the doctrines of Plato, the Thing-in-itself of Kant, the Absolute Knowing of Hegel, the Way of Laozi and Zhuangzi, the Heaven of Confucius and Mengzi, the Original State of Zen, and the Heavenly Principle of Zhu Xi and many others. For Wang Yangming, however, the universal substance of origin, able to generate all living things in heaven and earth and innate to the mind of man, was conscience.

In teaching us to concentrate upon conscience, Wang Yangming makes us grasp the significance of this spiritual source and use it to build an extensive inner connection with others, with heaven and earth, and with all living things. In this way, we may secure a solid foundation for our life and give peace to our spirit, thus bringing meaning to life and opening up a worthwhile way of living it. In the words of the ancient Chinese this is known as "bringing calm to the body and establishing life" and "once the fundamentals are established the Way will follow." Of course, it is impossible to scientifically prove the belief that there is a spiritual quality to the universe or that the life of man has a sacred or superior origin. Because this is a kind of belief, it also follows that upholding and respecting the lifestyle of the belief may also be termed a belief. A belief may not be proved or disproved; it is completely a matter of individual choice. You may believe that life in this vast and boundless universe is a temporary and insignificant existence, that the arrival of man in the world is purely incidental and that there is no particular meaning to living. Or you may believe that, even for just a moment's happiness, the origins of life are sacred and superior and that everyone who comes into

11

this world has the mission of perfecting their own character and realizing their potential in order to create value for society and for others, and to secure for themselves a high quality life of joy, happiness, and success.

Of course, if life could be reduced to the two propositions above, I think that the majority of people would choose the second. For humanity, the avoidance of suffering in favor of happiness and of disaster in favor of prosperity are profound natural demands. But how may these demands be satisfied? How may this joy, happiness, and success be sought? Even if it is not self-evident, it is a question worth deep consideration. If the ways in which we satisfy or seek these demands are defective or the direction we take is mistaken, then not only may we have paid a great price in the process of our search, it is also entirely possible that we have proceeded in the opposite direction, leading finally to the loss of the meaning of life, the collapse of life itself, and alienation of the spirit.

We should not deceive ourselves into thinking that we do not already exist in a society where material desires are rampant and that we are not already more or less in the predicament described above. In seeking its causes there are two basic points:

First, the excessive importance that we attach to material considerations and to money and the belief that joy, happiness, and success can be realized through material means has brought in its wake an expansion in material desire and an atrophy of spiritual life. These days, trapped by this kind of predetermined and singular lifestyle and concept of values, and fundamentally having lost our freedom of choice, we seem unable to dare think that there are other lifestyle possibilities. Herbert Marcuse (1898–1979), the American philosopher, called this: "One-dimensional man."

Second, the excessive importance that we place on the evaluations of society and the views of other people has led us to the point where we allow society and others to define our joy, happiness, and success, thereby ignoring our own true spiritual needs. Thus, as each individual is hijacked by a conspiracy of fashionable values and the collective subconscious, we lose our "self" and our character exhibits serious signs of "externalization." As the modern Confucian scholar Liang Shuming (1893–1988) put it, this is a life with an "external focus" in which it is very difficult to experience true joy and happiness. Even when you achieve a certain success, it is perhaps defined by the external world and not by what you yourself really wanted.

Of course, nobody can exist in this world without money and material. However, the crux of the problem lies in the fact that although both are necessary conditions for the attainment of joy, happiness, and success, they are by no means sufficient. That is to say, though it is true that without a certain material basis it is difficult to achieve joy, happiness, and success, even with such a basis there is no guarantee that they can be realized automatically. The reason being that despite the acquisition of so much of the material of the external life and despite the evaluations of others, in the end, the basic factor in determining our happiness or not is our own feelings and experience. To take it further, it is not only the somewhat internal experiences of joy and happiness that usually require spiritual health; even success, which is more reliant upon external factors, is intimately related to perfection of character and strength of spirit.

Consequently, if we wish to achieve spiritual health and strength and perfection of character, rather than continuing as a "one-dimensional man" with an external focus, we should undertake self-cultivation and the exercise of our conscience.

In the same way that the word "conscience" has two meanings (the fundamental substance of life and moral awareness), "exercise" has three: realization, expansion, and practice. Realization is the discovery of the conscience within us; expansion is the perfection of our character and the promotion of moral ability; and practice is the employment of conscience in our daily lives.

Conscience as the fundamental substance of life transcends all the phenomena of binary opposites, thus transcending good and evil. Hence, Wang Yangming speaks of "an entity with neither virtue nor evil intent"; but conscience in its role as the moral awareness of the inner mind has the ability to distinguish between good and evil, and so Wang Yangming also says: "Conscience is an awareness of good and evil."

Normally, nobody makes moral judgements about what we think, say, or do in our daily lives and we are generally negligent in this area. It is only when something that we have said or done produces consequences for good or ill that affect us directly or indirectly that we suddenly take notice. Thus, if we wish to implement Wang Yangming's School of Mind in our lives, there is no doubt that the essential starting point is the maintenance of an ever-present conscience in the way we treat people and in our attitude to things. In other words, we must preserve a distinct oversight and sense of every thought, word, and deed: "To know both the good of things and the bad of things and then to do that which should be done and cease that which should not be done."

This is the exercise of conscience and the only gateway to self-cultivation for Confucianism, Buddhism, and Daoism, the three schools of Chinese philosophy.

There is a feeling amongst some people that the presence of conscience is a restriction, but paradoxically, the seemingly independent life that we can see is restrained by invisible fetters: our senses are seduced by the brilliance of fashionable tastes that stimulate our desires and turn us willingly to loyal adherents of the worship of fetishes; in another way, the pervasive concepts of fashionable ideas encroach on our ability for independent thought and nudge us towards a slavish imitation of popular thought and lifestyles to the gradual loss of self. The apparent "restrictions" of the exercise of conscience in self-cultivation actually turn out to be the only way to spiritual independence. The reason for putting it like this is quite simple: a person must first be able to be the master of his own mind before he can attain spiritual health and be qualified for spiritual independence. If we lack the ability to master our own mind and are negligent in attending to our spirit, speech, and actions, then we will be easily hijacked by fashionable values and controlled by the outlook and assessment of others, disturbed by our own moods and desires and manipulated by external events. What kind of independence, pray, may such a man speak of?

Apart from this, some might say: might not the constant exercise of conscience make the act of proper living too exhausting?

True, in a certain sense self-cultivation is no easy matter. In fact, not only self-cultivation but everything worthwhile in life, such as work, study, establishing a business, and even managing a marriage or educating children, all demand the expenditure of great physical and mental effort and unremitting perseverance. This being so, how can we believe that the practice of Wang Yangming's School of Mind does not require either effort or devotion? In Wang Yangming's words, true self-cultivation "requires a bruise at every blow and blood from every slap" in order to lend strength to effort. The Zen masters of ancient China often compared self-cultivation to "growing a lotus in a furnace" or a "great life after a great death." Thus, we can see that truly significant self-cultivation must be, like rebirth in a bath of fire, an utter transformation of character and a spiritual nirvana.

There is absolutely no doubt that there is no shortcut to spiritual health and strength and perfection of character, it can only be achieved through painstaking self-cultivation. In all truth, the road to spiritual independence is not laid with flowers or red carpets but built with resolution and courage. I believe that if, from this moment on, you are willing to take responsibility for your own life and willing to step out on the path to reality, there will come a day when you will be able to find life's meaning and live a life of real value, in the end achieving a state of absolute spiritual independence in which "all that I desire falls within prescribed limits."

Part I

This Is How Sages Are Refined

In following the Way of the sages, one's own nature is sufficient of itself, those in the past who sought the ultimate principle in matters and things were in error.

Wang Yangming, Annual Chronicle

Wang Shouren, styled Boan, otherwise known as Yangming, a native of Yuyao County in Shaoxing Prefecture, Zhejiang Province (now Yuyao City in Zhejiang), was born in 1472 and died in 1529. Because he had lived as a hermit in the Yangming caves in the Kuaiji Hills in the southeast of Shaoxing County and had established the Yangming Academy, he was also known as Master Yangming.

Wang Yangming was a well-known philosopher, writer, and military expert of the Ming dynasty as well as a major and representative figure of the Neo-Confucian Rationalist School of the Song (960–1279) and Ming dynasties and the creator of the School of Mind. His official appointments included Minister of the Nanjing Ministry of War and Left Censor-in-Chief. He is one of a small handful of figures in Chinese history that combined in themselves the three incorruptible qualities of virtue, attainment, and power of expression, becoming a great Confucian who shattered the concepts of both past and present. His qualities of character and intellect wrote a glorious page not only in the history of Chinese philosophy, but also further afield in Japan, the Korean peninsula, and Southeast Asia where they had a deep and long-lasting influence on later generations.

The Skepticism of the Child Prodigy: Is Common Sense Reliable?

The young Wang Yangming was an exceptionally intelligent child. It is said that at the age of ten, when out with his grandfather on a hillside viewing the moon one evening, he suddenly burst out with the following poem:

> When the mountains are near
> And the moon is far,
> The moon feels small,
> And we say the mountains
> Are bigger than the moon.
> If man had the eyes of heaven,
> We would see that
> The mountains are small
> But the moon is huge.

The value of this little poem does not lie in whether or not it contains beauty of rhetoric or whether it is metrically correct but in its exceptional point of view and the flavor of the theory of relativity in its thinking.

The basis of this poem is the idea that people's awareness of things is limited by their position and point of observation, hence any judgement about things should be treated with skepticism. For example, an observer seated on a hill will feel that the hills around him are very large and the moon in the sky is very small; but if the observer was able to stand and look from the heavens he would see that in fact his hill was very small and the moon was very large. In that case, which judgement is true? In other words, what is the fundamental nature of things?

Whilst the child did not provide an answer, his idea gave us the following point of departure: man's powers of perception are limited and his awareness of things is relative, thus much of our common sense and knowledge does not stand the test of considered examination.

It is easy to see from this poem that from the beginning, Wang Yangming's perceptions of the world were strongly colored by subjectivism and skepticism and were very different from the views of the general run of people. In fact, looking at the history of Western philosophy it is not difficult to discover points of view similar to those of Wang Yangming. The 1st-century BC Greek philosopher Aenesidemus's famous Ten Tropes took aim at the relativity of man's cognitive abilities. His seventh Trope is practically the same as Wang Yangming's poem. He believed that the same object appeared differently by reason of distance and position. Large appeared small, square appeared round, straight appeared crooked, and ranges of hills that appeared smooth in the distance looked like the snaggled teeth of a dog at close quarters. Consequently, it is impossible to exclude the elements of position and placement and still be aware of an object. Its fundamental nature is unknowable.

Of course, at the age of ten, the young Wang Yangming's doubts about common sense were just based upon a precociously intelligent nature. It was impossible for there to have been mature and considered thought. But it was just this precocity that, by far, outstripped his immediate peers and even those of the same generation. In this sense, it is here that a clue emerges as to why, later, it was possible for Wang Yangming to defy conventional opinion and express such fierce doubts and judgements about the "Cheng-Zhu School of Reason" in official ideology and to overturn their idea of "seeking the ultimate reason in matters and things," and to establish in its place the theories of "there is no object outside the mind" and "there is no reason outside the mind" of the School of Mind.

The Path Towards Sagehood

Wang Yangming's father Wang Hua took first place in the imperial examinations of 1481 during the reign of the Ming Emperor Chenghua (1465–1487) and was appointed to the Hanlin Academy as a Senior Historiography Compiler where his achievements became well known. He had great expectations of his son and sought out the best private school in Beijing hoping that he would study diligently and that like his father his name would appear on the board of honor and he would take first place in the imperial examinations. To the father's surprise his son's performance caused him great disappointment. He showed no intention of studying and spent the days in rowdy behavior on the streets with friends.

On one occasion, Wang Yangming was caught red-handed by his father while playing about on the streets. Wang Hua sternly scolded him: "For generations our family has lived by learning and study, why is it that amusement has become second nature to you?"

Wang Yangming calmly wiped the dirt from his face and asked: "What's the point of study?"

Wang Hua said: "Study will enable you to become a great official. The reason I was able to come top in the exam was because I studied hard."

Wang Yangming asked: "If the father comes top do the sons and grandsons come top as well?"

Wang Hua said: "Good thinking, but it's only my generation, if you want to come top too you must study really hard!"

Wang Yangming giggled and said: "Just one generation, then there's nothing rare about coming top!"

Wang Hua was furious and rolled up his sleeve in preparation to giving him a beating. Yangming hurriedly covered his head with his hands and slipped away like a puff of smoke.

Several days later, the teacher at the school, hearing that Yangming had contradicted his father in public, sought him out for a private chat. Yangming then asked him: "If someone wants to do something with his life, what's the most important thing in all the world?"

The teacher was delighted and thinking that this child was beginning to make sense of things, quickly said: "To study and pass the exams and bring glory to the clan and one's ancestors, that is the most important thing in all the world."

Yangming thought earnestly for a moment and then suddenly shook his head and said this: "Passing difficult exams happens all the time, how can it be the most important thing in all the world?"

The teacher was momentarily at a loss for words and could only ask: "Then child, as you see it, what do you think the most important thing would be?"

Yangming thought again and then solemnly pronounced: "Only by becoming a sage may one achieve the most important thing."

When Wang Hua heard about this later he was both pleased and amused and remarked to Yangming: "How extravagant are the ambitions of children!"

Time passed and very soon Yangming was fifteen. He left Beijing and toured the Great Wall on horseback by himself. Standing on the lofty fortifications amongst the steep terrain, Wang Yangming gazed into the distance and saw only the blue of the hills and mountain ranges piled one upon the other and in a sudden flash, a wave of noble aspiration that encompassed rivers and embraced the world flooded into his inner consciousness. History records that this tour, during which he made a study of the customs and conditions of the people, paid homage to the battles of the past, and pondered the strategy of defending the border, "fired in him a passion to govern all." In fact, long before his tour of the Great Wall, when he was only fourteen, he had spent the days in the "practice of archery and riding and attention to military tactics" and reading all the ancient military treatises that he could find. The natural Chinese martial spirit and sense of chivalry never ever left him.

Following the fall of the Song dynasty (960–1279), China's scholar official class fell prey to the bad habit of "Standing idly with hands in sleeves discussing their inner nature when all was well, and merely promising the ruler to give their lives when confronted by danger." From an early age Wang Yangming conceived a bitter detestation for these useless and corrupt officials, thereby eventually encouraging himself through the application of a combination of morality and action, both cultivating self and helping others. Later, his forceful advocacy of the idea of the "unity of knowledge and action" was undertaken in the hope of using this strong, active, combined, and truly Confucian spirit to cure the shallow, chaotic, and hypocritical ills of the age.

In 1488 at the age of seventeen Wang Yangming, at his father's bidding, traveled to Nanchang in Jiangxi Province to marry a distant cousin. The following year, he returned to Yuecheng in Shaoxing with his bride. Passing through Shangrao he made a particular point of calling on the great Confucian master Lou Yizhai (1422–1491). The master was a loyal adherent of the Cheng-Zhu School of Reason who welcomed him enthusiastically and expounded the theory of "investigating things and extending knowledge." Wang Yangming was much enlightened, particularly by the master's final phrase: "Sages must study to achieve."

From then on it was this phrase that illuminated Wang Yangming's path towards sagehood. If one assumes that the question asked of the master at the private school: "What's the most important thing in all the world?" just derived from a kind of vague and not yet matured ability, then the ambition sparked by Master Lou's phrase about sages becomes without doubt a self-conscious and definite spiritual quest.

In 1492, the 21-year-old Wang Yangming passed the provincial exam and hurried to the capital to prepare for the metropolitan exams the following year. During his revision he read every book he could find by the 11th-century Neo-Confucian scholar Zhu Xi (1130–1200) and then thought hard about the meaning of Zhu's principle of "investigating things to seek out Principle." One day he was reading by the window and saw the phrase "There is fine and coarse in all things both within and without, every plant and tree, all contain reason." He raised his head and, by coincidence, seeing a small cluster of fresh green bamboos in the courtyard he decided to sit and meditate amongst them so as to seek out the heavenly logic that they contained.

Wang Yangming sat amongst the bamboos in meditation for seven days and nights. Not only was he unable to establish the Heavenly Principle within the bamboos, he also fell ill with exhaustion.

The utter defeat inflicted by the bamboos aroused a hitherto non-existent anxiety and doubt about Zhu Xi's theory of the examination of things: "If a few bamboos have examined me half to death, what is there that I can use to examine all matters and all objects?"

The Wang Yangming of the time, of course, did not dare express his doubts openly and could only take comfort from phrases such as "Even a sage must consider whether or not he has the talent."

Put plainly, in using this technique to examine the nature of things, Wang Yangming actually misunderstood Zhu Xi's original meaning. Zhu Xi's "investigating things to seek out Principle" meant conducting observation, research, and consideration of all matters and things in the life of nature and society in order to acquire knowledge and understanding of the universal and eternal "Principle" that they contained. There were two levels of meaning to this Principle: one referred to its arrangement, rules, and criteria; the other to the cosmic reason or cause that created all sentient beings in heaven and earth. Although in this context Principle is extremely abstract, there will come a day when, after a period of intense striving and through profound effort and unceasing study pursued with respect and sincerity, there will be a sudden moment of enlightenment.

It is easy to see that the Cheng-Zhu School of Reason pursued a gradualist approach to understanding while the temperamentally headstrong Wang Yangming unconsciously used the Zen Buddhist technique of sudden enlightenment in an attempt to achieve understanding at a single stroke by extracting the Principle of the reason of heaven from an examination of the bamboos. The result was, of course, a waste of effort.

Although the examination of the bamboos was a defeat, the spirit of perseverance that Wang Yangming showed in sticking to his search for truth was remarkable. The role of a sage is unlike doing business, in no way does each investment produce an immediate return. Rather, it is like a scientific experiment where each defeat is a step closer to success. At the time that Wang Yangming was exerting such effort, his spiritual environment had already developed beyond the normal and even if he had not transcended the commonplace and become a sage, he was certainly utterly different from the average person.

Do Not Waver, Maintain Your Inner Freedom

In 1493, Wang Yangming took the metropolitan exams and unfortunately failed. He tried again in 1496 and failed again. Fellow students who had failed over a number of years were despondent and thought it a matter of shame that they had studied hard for ten years and had failed repeatedly. Wang Yangming said: "People think failing the exam a matter of shame, I think wavering because of failure a matter of shame."

In this context, "wavering" refers to the negative state

of mind born of bitter experience and the subsequent way in which this negativity is allowed to control one's mental state. As Wang Yangming saw it, failing the exam was no failure, the real failure lay in allowing failure to engender a feeling of frustration that led to mental suffering and distress.

In short, not wavering and retaining motivation means maintaining one's inner freedom and always remaining master of one's own soul under whatever circumstances. This kind of formidable, independent spiritual strength is the "spirit of nobility" described by Mengzi.

The reason why man is superior to animals is first because of his ability to reason and next because of his possession of free will. Faced with an external stimulus, animals can only respond on the basis of a conditioned reflex but rational man is in no sense like this. There is a space between the stimulus and the response and that space is occupied by our strength and independence. That is to say that in the face of whatever external conditions or experience, we retain the power to determine our own attitude, point of view, and response, thus deciding on our actions rationally.

Modern neurological evidence demonstrates that when we alter our view of a situation our state of mind alters as well. Psychologically speaking it has also been demonstrated that the vast majority of negative states of mind arise not from the situation itself but from the view that we take of it. The American psychologist Maxwell Maltz once discussed his own secret way of maintaining internal independence

by separating view from fact. He believed that in order
to exert effective control of one's mental state it was
necessary to separate opinion or view from fact and the
reality of the situation from exaggerated obstacles and then
to construct our reactions and actions firmly upon the basis
of the facts themselves and not upon one's own views or
those of others. The distress suffered by Wang Yangming's
fellow students, despondent because of having failed their
exams, had been caused by the view of matters and things
that they had adopted. But because he had had the wisdom
to see through this, Wang Yangming did not waver in the
face of multiple failures and was able to maintain his inner
independence throughout.

The Cheng-Zhu School of Reason and
the Lu-Wang School of Mind

In 1499, the 28-year-old Wang Yangming took the
metropolitan exams for the third time and achieved
success at last, graduating in the first class with the title
of Metropolitan Graduate with Honor, and subsequently
occupying posts as Chief Examiner of Shandong Provincial
Examinations and Secretary of the Bureau of Military
Appointments. It was at this time that he struck up an
instantaneous and close friendship with the Hanlin Bachelor
Zhan Ruoshui (1466–1560). They were both dissatisfied at
the deep-rooted bureaucratic tendencies and formalization
of the Cheng-Zhu School and agreed to promote a genuine

study of the sages.

Wang Yangming had been determined to become a sage from his youth, but in many years of complications and setbacks had never achieved a fundamental breakthrough. He was filled with doubt and perplexity about what was the true study of the sages. However, it was through his relationship with Zhan Ruoshui that he achieved a major step towards understanding in the form of the School of Mind established by the great Confucian scholar of the Southern Song dynasty (1127–1279), Lu Jiuyuan (1139–1193).

Historically, the School of Reason represented by the two Chengs (Cheng Hao 1032–1085 and Cheng Yi 1033–1107) and Zhu Xi (1130–1200) is known as the "Cheng-Zhu School of Reason" while the School of Mind represented by Lu Jiuyuan and later Wang Yangming is known as the Lu-Wang School of Mind. In broad terms, both schools belong to the Song-Ming School of Reason; but taking a narrower definition the School of Reason and the School of Mind belong to two different sects and differ substantially in matters of academic ideology and religious practice.

In scholarship and religious practice, the Cheng-Zhu School of Reason emphasized "investigating things and extending knowledge," that is to seek out Principle through things: "Every object possesses its Principle that must be sought out." This is an emphasis on the importance of study and knowledge, a belief that the moral state gradually improves through advances in knowledge. Consequently, Zhu Xi quite clearly advocated: "Investigating things to seek out Principle, that is man's ladder to sagehood." He believed that if scholars failed to tread this path seriously and indulged in mystery and meditation it would lead to shallowness of intellect and arrogance of character.

Lu Jiuyuan was the precise opposite of Zhu Xi. He quoted Mengzi to the effect that most important in learning was the necessity to first confirm that man's original mind was the fundamental form of everything in the cosmos and at the same time the source of all moral ethics. Only in this way would it be possible to avoid being confused by all matters and all objects. Moreover, to vainly expend effort in seeking externally, while ignorant both of the original mind and the fundamental body, would be to make learning and self-cultivation "water without a source."

Clearly, in Lu Jiuyuan's view, an extension of knowledge could not lead directly to the perfection of the character of man. Just following the line of Cheng and Zhu would result in falling into the predicament of "Engaging with the outside but neglecting the inside, being erudite and knowledgeable but with no grasp of the essentials." By contrast, if it were possible to know the original form of the life of the cosmos without departing from one's original mind then all the learning of the sages would naturally be available within that mind. It was on the basis of this perception that Lu Jiuyuan advanced the proposition that "Mind is Principle" thereby establishing the rival School of Mind in competition with the Cheng-Zhu School of Reason.

The simplicity and straightforwardness of Lu's School of Mind approach came like rain in a drought to Wang

Yangming who had struggled unsuccessfully to enter the gate of enlightenment for so long. For him, encountering the School of Mind was a true stroke of fortune. However, since the School of Reason had been adopted as official dogma, the School of Mind had been marginalized. It was this historical encounter with Wang Yangming that reignited the flame of the School of Mind after several hundred years of silence and led to the birth of the Yangming School of Mind.

Enlightenment at Longchang: the Birth of the Yangming School of Mind

In 1505, Zhu Houzhao (1491–1521), then barely fifteen, succeeded to the throne. Enthroned as the Ming Emperor Wuzong (reigned 1505–1521), Zhu Houzhao was extremely fond of the eunuch Liu Jin (1451–1510) and others, allowing them to wantonly interfere in government and trade in titles and positions. The civil officials, led by the Deputy Minister of the Cabinet Office, were outraged and jointly memorialized the throne urging that Liu Jin and his associates should be put to death.

Zhu Houzhao totally ignored the memorial. Liu Jin then began his counter attack and had the civil officials successively flogged in the palace courtyard and some even sent into exile. Wang Yangming was amongst them and received forty strokes of the heavy bamboo, followed by imprisonment, expulsion from court, and exile to Guizhou as sub-postmaster at Longchang.

In the spring of 1507, Wang Yangming started his journey into remote exile to become a very minor official at the post station in that desolate place. His only subordinate was an elderly grey-haired post-runner; the sole property of which he had charge was the dilapidated post station. Worst of all, despite his status as sub-postmaster, Wang Yangming did not have the right to live in the post station since under court regulations exiled officials were not permitted to live in official premises. All he could do was to build a hut nearby and live there with his followers. Later he found a cave at Longgang Hill, three *li* from the post station, something that might be considered a refuge from wind and rain.

In fact, Wang Yangming found no difficulty in living under such difficult and dangerous conditions since immersion over the years in the way of sagehood had tempered him and even if he had not yet become a sage, he was very different from the normal run of people. Consequently, the suffering and poverty of life was of no concern, but with him all the time was that fundamental problem that had occupied his mind for most of his life: how do you become a sage?

In an attempt to achieve comprehension of the way of the sages, Wang Yangming meditated day and night and in the course of time his spirit gradually eased and became clearer. Later, his speculation moved on from the problems of loss and gain, insult and honor, leaving only the question of "life and death a single concept" unresolved. He built himself a stone coffin in which he meditated on the proposition "if a sage can be in this position, can there be any Way?"

Eventually his effort paid off, when meditating in the silent depths of night he suddenly achieved enlightenment. History records that at the moment of enlightenment he leaped wildly from the coffin shouting and frightened his followers.

Erich Fromm described enlightenment in the following terms: "One's eyes are suddenly opened; oneself and the world appear in a different light, are seen from a different viewpoint. There is usually a good deal of anxiety aroused before the experience takes place; while afterwards a new feeling of strength and certainty is present."[1] Although what Fromm was describing was the state of Zen enlightenment, it is possible to say that on this basis Wang Yangming's enlightenment at Longchang was identical.

At this point, as far as Wang Yangming is concerned, although mountains remain mountains and water is still water and the Longchang post-station is still what it is, he has already been reborn into a new universe. In an instant,

[1] Translator's Note: The author has quoted a number of texts translated into Chinese from their original language, usually English. Where possible, the original text is reproduced and identified as such. Where this has not been possible, I have re-translated back into English from Chinese accepting that although the general meaning may match the original, the precise wording may not.

the suffering, perplexity, and bewilderment disappear and it is as if he has never existed before.

Heaven and earth, self and mind, all one glorious whole!

Then, what really is it that Wang Yangming realized in that deep cave in Longchang? In a sentence it is: "In beginning to know the Way of the sages, one's own nature is sufficient of itself, those in the past who sought the ultimate Principle in matters and things were in error."

In modern terms, the Way of the sages is a means and process of self-maturity, self-perfection, and self-realization and a sage is a person who is fulfilling his potential and is approaching perfection of character. "One's own nature sufficient of itself" is not to say that one has been a sage from the start but that one's nature contains all the potential to become a sage. Later scholars who followed the Wang school often spoke of "streets full of sages" in a reference to this potential. It is precisely because this potential has been in one's possession from the very beginning that it is an absolute mistake to seek the means and way of sagehood externally amongst "matters and things."

Wang Yangming's exclamation of enlightenment marked both the end of his 20-year intellectual search in the Cheng-Zhu School of Reason and the point of departure for the logic of the whole of the Wang Yangming School of Mind. It marks the moment when the two schools parted company.

Following his enlightenment, he was invited to deliver lectures at the Wenming College in Guiyang and began to reveal his theory of the "unity of knowledge and action."

In 1510, Liu Jin fell from favor and Wang Yangming returned to government. Thereafter the School of Mind obtained many adherents and its theories were widely discussed thus beginning its transmission throughout the empire.

In 1516, Wang Yangming was promoted to the post of Left Censor-in-Chief and concurrently Grand Co-Ordinator of Southern Jiangxi where he put down rebellions in the provinces of Fujian, Jiangxi, Hubei and Hunan, and Guangdong. Whilst in Jiangxi he started to advocate his theory of the "application of conscience."

In 1519, he was dispatched to Fujian to put down a mutiny and when he reached Fengcheng, hearing that Zhu Chenhao (1476–1521) the Prince of Ning had rebelled, he raised an army and put down the rebellion within 43 days. His fame grew from then on and two years later he was appointed Minister of the Nanjing Ministry of War and Count of Xinjian.

In 1528, Wang Yangming put down disturbances at Si'en and Tianzhou in Guangxi and in the same year requested permission to retire because of illness, dying on the way to his ancestral home at the age of 57. As he lay dying one of his followers asked him if he had any last words. He smiled and replied, "The mind is glorious, what further words are needed" and then expired.

In 1568, on the 40th anniversary of Wang Yangming's death, the Ming Emperor Muzong (reigned 1566–1572), also named Zhu Zaihou (1537–1572), gave his assessment of Wang Yangming as "Armed with righteousness, the great man of his generation, skilled in bringing order out of chaos and extending strategies to save the dynasty and bring comfort to the people."

Two hundred years later, the great Qing dynasty (1644–1911) scholar Zhang Tingyu (1672–1755) and others who were compiling the *History of the Ming Dynasty* wrote: "In the later years of the Ming dynasty there was nobody amongst court officials who resembled Yangming in his ability to achieve military victory."

After Wang Yangming, the School of Mind was developed into the theory of the age by his followers such as Wang Gen, Wang Ji, Qian Dehong and others. It had a deep influence on the history of Chinese thought over the next five hundred years. In the Ming dynasty and throughout the Qing dynasty and even into the Republic, Wang Yangming was idolized by many politicians, thinkers and the well-intentioned classes who worshipped the theories of the School of Mind and found them an inexhaustible source of spiritual strength.

The School of Mind crossed the sea to Japan at the end of the Ming dynasty where it gathered many admirers and had a profound influence on the Meiji Restoration and the modernization of Japan. In Japan today, many industrialists of the first rank regard it as a guiding light.

In recent years, following the revival of traditional culture in China, there has been an upsurge in the study of Wang Yangming's School of Mind in the worlds of politics and commerce, in intellectual circles, and even in popular society. Just as Du Weiming (1940–), the new Confucius of the present age, said: "For the last five hundred years the living spring of Confucianism has been Wang Yangming and the 21st century will be his century."

To understand the wisdom of the School of Mind you must read its representative work, the *Instructions for Practical Living* (*Chuanxi Lu*). The *Instructions* was compiled by Wang Yangming's followers from records of his conversations and letters. It is divided into three volumes and was edited by Xu Ai, Lu Cheng, Xue Kan, Nan Daji, and Qian Dehong. The *Instructions* contains Wang Yangming's major philosophical ideas and is a Confucian classic that had profound influence on later generations. This author has collected its essence with the aim of breaking Wang Yangming's spiritual code and allowing the reader, through coming to understand the wisdom of the School of Mind and grasping its essential spirit, to gain an effective experience of life, realize his fundamental potential, and gain a life of wisdom, joy, happiness and beauty.

Part II

Mind Is Reason: The Road to Self-Realization Lies in the Mind

Zhu Xi believed that *li* (Reason or Principle) was the universal essence of substance that derived from all sentient beings of heaven and earth; hence it was perpetual and objective and whether or not mankind existed, or was aware of the Principle, it was always there. Considered this way, this Heavenly Principle was only a moral standard that existed outside self and the foundations of the perfection of man's character and of self-realization were not based upon the inner self mind. Consequently, even if one were educated to become a sage, it was just a process of passive compliance with a set of established social values. It was here that the concepts of man's basic nature and basic consciousness were seriously weakened. As Wang Yangming saw it, the Principle was a function of the self-mind and there was no need to borrow it from outside. Put another way, the moment one became aware of mind, it was possible to see that the potential and energy to become a sage had always existed within one's own being. Consequently, perfection of character and self-realization were a responsibility that arose from "self" and "being" (because you were a goldmine and must therefore necessarily become gold). At the same time, they were a privilege bestowed by heaven (no external circumstances could deprive you of the innate quality of your gold). Hence it was from here that man's qualities of initiative, self-confidence, and creativity were vigorously developed and displayed in their entirety.

Chapter 1
Trees and Flowers Amongst the Rocks: Wang Yangming's Worldview

Xu Ai said:"To seek virtue only in the mind, then I fear there would be many things under heaven that we would be unable to understand completely."

Master Yangming replied:"Mind is Principle. Do you mean to say that heaven can possess matter or Principle that is outside the mind?"

Instructions for Practical Living, Vol. I, Xu Ai's Record

Xu Ai (1488–1518), a native of Yuhang in Zhejiang Province, was Wang Yangming's brother-in-law and his first pupil.

The proposition that "Mind is Principle" is the inalienable core of Wang Yangming's School of Mind. It is also the point at which the School of Mind and the School of Reason part company. Before we go on to elucidate Wang Yangming's proposition, we should first see how Zhu Xi understood and defined the concepts of Mind and Reason/Principle.

So far as Zhu Xi was concerned, Reason or Principle was the universal essence of substance derived from all sentient beings of heaven and earth: "Principle is the way of the metaphysical and the very basis of life." Metaphysicality is the state of things before they have taken form and of the time when the sentient beings of heaven and earth had not yet been formed. Zhu Xi said that Principle was the "Way" of the as yet unformed sentient beings of heaven and earth. It is the equivalent of saying that Principle is perpetual, transcendent, and abstract.

Then what is Mind? Zhu Xi said: "Mind is the perception and feeling of man, it controls the body and responds to all things and objects." A further sentence adds: "When it refers to the personal self of form and energy it is known as the mind of man; when it refers to Heavenly Principle, it is known as the mind of the Way." Thus, for Zhu Xi, the process of the perfection of man's character was through the operation of Heavenly Principle, turning the mind of man to the mind of the Way.

Precisely because Zhu Xi believed that Principle was abstract, perpetual, incorporeal, and intangible, and transcended the individual, it was something that the mind of man could not immediately grasp, hence man had to "investigate things to seek out Principle" and venture amongst matters and things to retrieve that Heavenly Principle.

But for Wang Yangming, Mind, of course, primarily referred to perception: "Mind is not a lump of flesh, it is the seat of all perception. For example, the awareness, sight, and hearing of eyes and ears, the awareness of pain and itching in hands and feet, it is these perceptions that constitute mind" (*Instructions for Practical Living, Vol. III*).

However, the fundamental difference between Zhu Xi and Wang Yangming lay in the fact that the latter did not separate Mind into two, the mind of man and the mind of the Way, but believed that this single mind was the Heavenly Principle. As Wang Yangming saw it, the mind with which you could at once experience directly, the mind that could see, listen, speak, and act was the essence of the substance of all sentient beings of heaven and earth and the universal prime principle that transcended time and space.

Since the mind of man was indivisible from the Heavenly Principle and constituted a unity of man with heaven, did not distinguish between ancient and modern, and completely filled the universe, then, naturally, there was neither matter nor Principle outside the mind. In other words, the path to perfection of character and self-realization was not external and did not lie outside but lay within the minds of us all, if we dared to take it on and were willing to put it into practice.

"If one believes that all may reach sagehood then naturally one has the confidence to do so!" (*Instructions for Practical Living, Vol. III*)

This is the essential core value at the heart of Wang Yangming's School of Mind and one of his most important legacies, the establishment of subjective experience and the promotion of a subjective self-awareness.

In Zhu Xi's context, the Heavenly Principle was a universal moral standard that existed outside self, thus the basis of perfection of character was not rooted in the inner mind of the self and even if one were taught to become a sage it was merely passive obedience to a predetermined set of social values. However, for Wang Yangming the potential and ability to become a sage existed within one's own life. Consequently, the perfection of character and self-realization was an innate obligation upon the self (because you were a gold-mine you had to become gold); at the same time it was also a power bestowed by heaven (no external circumstances could deprive you of the intrinsic quality of your gold). Hence it was from here that man's qualities of initiative, self-confidence, and creativity were vigorously developed and displayed in their entirety.

The origins of the basic difference between Zhu Xi and Wang Yangming lie in philosophical epistemology. Zhu Xi emphasized the objectivity of the external world in our thinking, but Wang Yangming harbored doubts about objectivity: once stripped of man's cognitive ability and observation, would the objectivity of the external world still stand? In other words, although we all occupy the same world, is my awareness of the world exactly the same as yours?

We have to realize that in the relationship between the cognitive system of man and the external world, man's intelligence is not an empty sheet of A4 paper, nor is our cognitive ability a photocopier. It cannot exactly copy every matter and thing of the external world into our intelligence. Immanuel Kant, the 18th-century German philosopher, laboriously elaborated proof of this and finally concluded that the internal structure of our intelligence determined the content of what we can know.

It is not difficult to discover through everyday experience that man's intelligence is rather like the paint and canvas of an artist, and that cognitive ability is the brush. Different people will have a different response, sense, and experience of the same object or circumstances. Consequently, each of us creates in the mind a "work of art" that differs from that of others.

To take a slightly imperfect example. There is an apple before us, and as you see it, it is a fruit that can supplement your vitamin intake. However, in the eyes of an insect it is a garden and granary; in the eyes of a stallholder it is a commodity that may be exchanged for money; in the eyes of a biologist it is a collection of cells; in the eyes of a physicist it is a pile of atoms, molecules, and electrons; the Christian will think of Eve and mankind's original sin; Newton will look and discover gravity; Steve Jobs will take a bite and the whole world will be filled with Apple fans mad for the iPad and iPhone. Since just a mere apple can produce so many differing perceptions, what about the whole world itself? Can this diverse and complicated world be absolutely the same to over seven billion people? In other words, can you say what an apple should be like in itself or what the world should be like in itself?

I think you cannot.

Similarly, I cannot either.

From this we may see that man's perception of the external world is by no means just a passive acceptance of information about the external world by the sensory organs but a process in which the cognitive element projects our intellect, experience, sense, attitudes, and feelings on to the target object, thus forming man's active awareness. In other words, this is a process in which man may, through the agency of his own cognition and awareness, "humanize" the material nature of the external world, or perhaps symbolize or signify it.

The ability of human society to cast off its primitive state and develop civilization is due to the development of language, writing, art, philosophy, religion, and science. If mankind had not "symbolized" the material nature of the external world through these cultural activities, there is no way that civilization could have been spread, inherited, or developed. Ernst Cassirer, the early 20th-century German philosopher, said: "Hence, instead of defining man as an *animal rationale*, we should define him as an *animal symbolicum*."

The symbolization of nature is basically a process in which man, through his active awareness, bestows a kind of "meaning" on the world. The late 19th-century Austrian psychologist Alfred Adler said: "But no human being can escape meanings. We experience reality always through the meaning we give it; not in itself, but as something interpreted."

On the basis of the sense of the frequently quoted saying: "In the eyes of a thousand readers there are a thousand Hamlets" we might perhaps say that as more than seven billion people live on this planet, it is the equivalent of the existence of more than seven billion different worlds.

Were it thus, would not the objective independence of the external world be overthrown?

If what Wang Yangming advocated was this kind of worldview then is he not a subjective idealist? In saying "there is nothing outside the Mind" and "there is no Principle outside the Mind" can he be denying the existence of the objective world?

Let us be in no hurry to reach a conclusion for the moment and see first what modern science has to say.

In the era of Newtonian physics, everybody believed that the world that surrounded them existed independently and that it was made up of various objects (tables, chairs, planets, atoms, and so on). Whether we observe them or not these objects continue to exist. This remains the world view and general knowledge of the vast majority of people. In Newtonian mechanics and general knowledge, the dimensions, form, and mass of a table are fixed attributes and do not alter depending upon whether we look at them or not, or look at them as we stand or as we run.

Thereafter, following the emergence of Einstein's Theory of Relativity, problems appeared for the objective reality of matter. According to the Theory of Relativity, when you observed a table from a standing posture its dimensions and shape and mass were not the same as when you observed it from a running posture. That is to say that the same object differed in length, form, and mass according to the observer and the conditions under which it was observed. Theoretically, the results of such observations may be limitless in number and each one may be real.

Since mass may "morph" at will according to differing conditions of observation, can there be any "independently existing" objective attributes to speak of?

In macroscopic measurement the emergence of the Theory of Relativity destroyed the idea of the attribute of "absolute objectivity" and quantum mechanics, which followed closely on its heels, completely overthrew the basic reality of mass in the field of sub-atomic measurement.

Before the birth of quantum mechanics, people believed that all matter strictly adhered to the three principles of Newtonian mechanics. For example, planets revolved in orbit, bullets traveled towards their target along an accurate path, and the internal structure of the atom was considered a miniature solar system—electrons swiftly circled the core of the atom rather as planets circled the sun. Subsequently, in 1913 the young Danish physicist Niels Bohr suddenly advanced the theory that there was no distinct orbit of travel for electrons and that they traveled along one orbit one moment and along another the next and that this sort of jump did not need any space in which to occur. This is to say that mass may suddenly leap from a state of nothing to a state of something and in reverse. We cannot know the concrete laws of movement for electrons, nor those for all known micro particles, including atoms. Frankly speaking, the hard solidity of the mass of our daily experience had become a crowd of insubstantial ghosts scattered at random.

This epoch-making scientific discovery was the well-

47

known "quantum jump."

In 1926, Niels Bohr's pupil Heisenberg further proposed that it was impossible to know simultaneously the position of an atom or electron and how it would move. Not only was it impossible to know, the concept of the determination of the position and momentum of atoms was without significance. One might ask an atom where it was and receive an answer, one might also ask an atom how it was moving and receive an answer, but it was impossible to know both answers at the same time.

This was Heisenberg's uncertainty principle, a basic theory of quantum mechanics.

Bohr put it bluntly: "The fuzzy and nebulous world of the atom only sharpens into concrete reality when an observation is made. In the absence of an observation, the atom is a ghost. It only materializes when you look for it."

This perplexed Einstein who said indignantly: "God does not play dice with the universe," thereafter rejecting quantum mechanics. Bohr was unperturbed, merely remarking: "If quantum mechanics hasn't profoundly shocked you, you haven't understood it yet."

In quantum mechanics the major characteristic of sub-atomic particles is described as "wave-particle duality": an electron or photon may sometimes exhibit the characteristics of a particle and at other times the characteristics of a wave. The determination of whether it is a wave or a particle is made through experimentation and observation. When it exhibits as a particle it is a little piece of concentrated matter, you may understand it as a tiny gurgling sphere. In its wave state it is a kind of formless momentum that can expand or disappear.

How is it that something can be both a particle and a wave? Can it be that the real, actual, battered chair in which I am sitting is made up of a phantom cloud of ghostly atoms?

In terms of quantum mechanics, I can only say: "Yes."

In 1935 in order to explain this "twin possibility" state visually, the 20th-century Austrian physicist and one of the founders of quantum mechanics, Erwin Schrödinger, designed a rather cruel but imaginary experiment. A cat is placed in a box with a flask of poison controlled by a device that triggers the release of the poison when radioactive decay is detected. Before the observer starts observation, it is impossible to determine whether radioactive decay has occurred, so the probability of the release of poison from the flask is 50 percent. This means that at any one time the unfortunate cat is in a state of "superposition" being both alive and dead and dead and alive. It requires the presence of an observer to open the box to determine whether the cat is dead or alive. Once you see it, it is either completely dead or completely alive.

This is the famous *Schrödinger's Cat* experiment. In fact, however, Wang Yangming had described a similar idea 400 years earlier.

Wang Yangming's idea derived from a story with the delightful name of *Trees and Flowers amongst the Rocks*.

> The master was touring Nan Zhen when a friend pointed to some trees and flowers growing amongst

the rocks and asked: "There is nothing under heaven that exists outside the mind, but these trees and flowers that blossom and fall in the deep hills, what relation do they have to my mind?"

The master said: "At the time when you had not seen the flowers, they existed in solitude with your mind. When you saw them, their color was momentarily obvious. Thus, you know that the flowers do not exist outside your mind." (*Instructions for Practical Living, Vol. III*)

In Wang Yangming's view, when a flower blossoms and falls by itself in the hills as yet unobserved by anybody, it is in a state of "latency" (the "solitude" of the story) similar to the cat with twin possibilities in Schrödinger's experiment, its shape and color only becoming "momentarily obvious" when someone comes to look at it, the instant in which the state of superposition changes to an eigenstate.

When they read this story, I do not think that any physicist or scientist who accepts the quantum theory, or any ordinary reader, will think that Wang Yangming was ridiculous. Nor will they simply regard him as a "subjective idealist" because the philosophical ideas enshrined in *Trees and Flowers amongst the Rocks* are totally at one with the fundamental principles of the theory of quantum mechanics. The well-known physicist Paul Davies said: "the commonsense view of the world, in terms of objects that really exist 'out there' independently of our observations, totally collapses in the face of the quantum factor." John

Wheeler, the physicist who coined the term "black hole," claimed that: "The precise nature of reality has to await the participation of a conscious observer."

In this sense, Wang Yangming's philosophical ideology and the discoveries of modern science might be described as singing a different tune from the same notation. Actually, Wang Yangming's worldview is not idealistic, nor materialistic, but a complete entity uniting both mind and matter. In fact, the contemporary scientific worldview is also striving to construct a holistic theory, for example, the statement of the quantum mechanics physicist David Bohm that: "The primary emphasis is now on undivided wholeness, in which the observing instrument is not separated from what is observed." Bohm used this in response to Heisenberg's statement: "The common division of the world into subject and object, inner world and outer world, body and soul is no longer adequate."

We can see from this that Wang Yangming's statement that "there is no matter outside the Mind, and no Principle outside the Mind" is not a denial of the existence of an objective world, or an attempt to deny objective rules or the laws of nature, but an attempt to demonstrate that any rule, law, or matter cannot exist independently of the cognition and observation of man. Similarly, human consciousness also cannot exist independently of these things. In Wang's words: "The Principle of things does not lie outside the self-mind. Seek the Principle outside the mind and there will be no Principle; leave aside the Principle to seek the self-mind, then what is the self-mind?" (*Instructions for Practical Living, Vol. II*)

Chapter 2
Creating a Secret Chamber for Your Soul

*One cannot say that every ordinary person possesses "the harmony of unexpressed emotion (*zhong*)." Substance and effect derive from the same source, once there is substance it follows that there must be effect. If there is a harmony of unexpressed emotion then presumably there must be a harmony of "expressed emotion (*he*)." The people of today cannot possess this harmony of expressed emotion and one should understand that the harmony of unexpressed emotion is also unachievable.*

Instructions for Practical Living, Vol. I, Record of Lu Cheng

In a situation where the human emotions of joy, anger, sorrow, and happiness have yet to be expressed, one's inner mind maintains a state of tranquility and harmony known as *zhong*; when the emotions are expressed they may, with a suitable measure of intensity, conform with natural law and the norms of society and ethics in a state known as *he*. The concepts of *zhong* and *he* occupy an extremely elevated realm. In the eyes of the Confucians, once society could universally achieve the realm of *zhonghe* both heaven and earth would be stabilized and proceed in perpetual motion and all sentient beings would develop and grow in their respective places.

Clearly, this can only be an ideal.

In all truth, how many of those beings entangled in the red dust of mundane life can both achieve *zhong*, the harmony of unexpressed emotion, and *he*, the harmony of appropriately expressed emotion, is a matter of considerable doubt. Particularly when you consider the modern generation, the pace of whose life is increasingly frenetic, whose occupational burdens are ever heavier and anxieties ever more numerous: who amongst them in their daily intercourse with others can guarantee that their mood and attitude will conform with societal norms and be appropriate? Even when nothing is the matter, who can guarantee that their own inner mind can maintain a state of "tranquility and harmony"?

There was a monk who asked the Zen Master Huihai of the Tang dynasty (618–907): "How may I use diligence in the practice of the Way?"

Huihai replied: "Eat when hungry, sleep when tired."

The monk said doubtfully: "Isn't everybody like that? Can it be that they are as diligent as the master?"

Huihai said: "Not the same."

The monk asked: "How is it not the same?"

Huihai said: "When he eats, he is unwilling to eat, for he is beset by multifold demands, when he sleeps, he is unwilling to sleep for he is turning over too many stratagems in his mind. So, it's not the same."

Think for yourself, how often in your recollection have you been able to eat a meal and carefully taste the flavor of each dish without there being too many demands upon you. When have you ever gone to bed and slept well without there being too many stratagems revolving in your head?

If, like Master Huihai, you can eat when hungry and sleep when tired, you may not possess the wisdom of a

Zen practitioner but at the very least you will enjoy the happiness of an ordinary person. Regrettably, most people in modern society cannot do this. In the words of Wang Yangming: "People today, when they eat, may have nothing in prospect but their mind is always unquiet and for this reason they have become accustomed to being busy and are thus unable to hold back." (*Instructions for Practical Living, Vol. III*)

What we chew when we eat is not food but all the many problems at work and the troubles of life; what we gain when we sleep is not rest but the memories and remorse of the past or the plans and anxieties for the future, or dissatisfaction and apprehension about the present. The "multifold demands" demonstrate our skill in cramming a plethora of things into our inner mind with the result that our spirit becomes a recycling center stuffed with rubbish. The "too many stratagems" show how we are always reckoning profit and loss so that we turn our lives into a dull financial report.

This is the misery of the modern generation.

It may be that on this point the happiness score of the ancients was rather higher than ours, though fundamentally there is little difference. For "When the empire prospers all come for profit and when it is in chaos they all leave for profit." As long as one remains living in the red dust of the mundane world it will be very difficult to attain the tranquility and harmony of the state of unexpressed emotion and difficult, too, to reach the state where the emotions of joy, anger, sorrow, and happiness are appropriately expressed.

As Zhu Xi explained it, the harmony of as yet unexpressed emotion is the essence of the substance of life, hence, it will be enough to put the effort of the practice of the Way into "effect," that is, the appropriate expression of joy, anger, sorrow, and happiness.

However, Wang Yangming believed that the internal essence of substance and external effect beat as one heart: the fact that in actual life, for many people, the failure of the external expression of state of mind to reach an appropriate suitability was evidence of defects in their inner state, that is to say, that the essence of substance still suffered a degree of obstruction. Thus, to state that ordinary people possessed "the inner harmony of unexpressed emotion" was inappropriate. In other words, the focus of self-cultivation for scholars should be directly upon the internal state and the elimination of obstructions from the body of the mind and not just upon external social relationships.

It is easy to see that the differences between Wang Yangming and Zhu Xi on this point constituted one of the fundamental divergences between Zhu's School of Reason and Wang's School of Mind.

As Zhu Xi saw it, Reason was external and effort should naturally be expended externally.

In Wang Yangming's eyes, Mind was Reason and the stabilization of the mind was fundamental.

If Zhu Xi and Wang Yangming had been two environmentalists, intent upon controlling the pollution of a river, Zhu Xi would probably have visited the river every day to remove the rubbish and drain away the polluted water. Despite all his painstaking industry his results would have been minimal, twice the effort for half the result. Wang Yangming would have proceeded straight upstream to close the factory that discharged its polluted effluent and tipped its rubbish into the river, and then returned to clean up the river, half the effort for twice the result and utterly relaxed.

There can be no doubt at all that what we need is Wang Yangming's way of doing things.

That factory producing pollution 24 hours a day is our own mind. If we never repair or clean out the "inner harmony of unexpressed emotion" then the states of mind that we display and the external actions of our behavior can, in the main, only be so much rubbish and sewage.

"If your heart is a volcano, how shall you expect flowers to bloom in your hands?" (Khalil Gibran)

Consequently, if we wish to retain a suitable moderation in our state of mind and behavior and to cease creating rubbish for ourselves or polluting the external world, there is one thing that has to be done from now on.

We must protect our spiritual environment.

Our starting point must be the harmony of unexpressed emotion.

What the ancients termed the harmony of unexpressed emotion is in fact what can, in modern language, be described as the serenity, tranquility, and calm of the inner mind. How can one achieve all this in a life tangled like dough twists and ever-turning activity?

The answer is as difficult or simple as you wish to make

it: it is to make a secret chamber for one's spirit.

Liang Qichao (1873–1929), the modern Chinese thinker, said: "He who studies to become a great man should in a lifetime spend some years living in the world beyond the world; should in the space of a year spend some months living in the world beyond the world; should in the length of a day spend some moments living in the world beyond the world."

The so-called "world beyond the world" does not refer to the moon or Mars nor to the Buddhist paradise of the Pure Land but to one's own spiritual life and inner being— as long as you are prepared to pause and reflect, you may free yourself from the restless clamor of life and enter a transcendent and tranquilly self-assured secret chamber of the spirit.

Why is a secret chamber of the spirit necessary?

Liang Qichao said that historically there had never been a "confused and muddle-headed" brain that could "carry through grand projects or establish great enterprises." For all "Heroes and great men, the burden of affairs become heavier and heavier and social relationships ever more complicated and numerous," thus there had to be a "world beyond the world to nurture the soul." Consequently, only those who understood how to create a spiritual secret chamber for themselves and could, from time to time, enter it for a moment, would achieve "clarity and purity of mind and a god-like strength of will."

How does one create a secret chamber of the spirit?

Answer: find an isolated time for oneself in which to

abandon for the moment the restraints and concerns of the world and enter one's inner mind and genuinely confront the inner self that has been forgotten by reality for so long. Then do something spiritual like meditating or practicing Zen, listening to music that moves the spirit, watching inspirational films, reading books by authors of wisdom and knowledge. Try to deepen and develop an interest and feeling for the things of the spirit and humanities such as literature, art, aesthetics, philosophy, psychology, and religion. Over time, you will be able to build yourself a calm, rich inner world that is not just pragmatic or utilitarian, thus creating a brand-new inner self and rebuilding your relationship with the outside world.

This is the secret chamber of the spirit and Liang Qichao's "world beyond the world." As one looks at the religious history of the world it is not difficult to see that Sakyamuni's becoming a Buddha, the teachings of Jesus, and the revelations of Mohammed all derived from the years of life and the months of years living in a "world beyond the world." Sakyamuni on the banks of the Nairanjana river, Jesus in the wilderness by the river Jordan, Mohammed in the cave of Hira: these were all indispensable secret chambers of the spirit, much as the post office at Longchang was for Wang Yangming.

From the age of nineteen, Steve Jobs, leader of the worldwide Apple cult before whom fans prostrated themselves, had a spiritual world comprised of elements of oriental feeling, Buddhist Zen, spiritual meditation, and intuitive experience that transcended the external environment. From this inner world, Steve Jobs obtained a new vision with which to observe the world and an astonishing ability to change it. In a certain sense, the reason that Steve Jobs has become a contemporary legend and Apple products have become a synonym for creativity, imagination, the pursuit of perfection, and inexhaustible passion, derives from Steve Jobs's unusual inner world and spiritual life.

Steve Jobs has been dead for several years, but he talked about his visit to India when he was nineteen and the influence that it had on his life:

> "The people in the Indian countryside don't use their intellect like we do, they use their intuition instead, and their intuition is far more developed than in the rest of the world. Intuition is a very powerful thing, more powerful than intellect, in my opinion. That's had a big impact on my work.
>
> Coming back after seven months in Indian villages, I saw the craziness of the Western world as well as its capacity for rational thought. If you just sit and observe you will see how restless your mind is. If you try to calm it, it only makes it worse, but over time it does calm, and when it does, there's room to hear more subtle things—that's when your intuition starts to blossom and you start to see things more clearly and be in the present more. Your mind just slows down and you see a tremendous expanse in the moment. You see so much more than you could see before. It's a discipline; you have to

practice it.

Zen has been a deep influence on my life ever since. At one point I was thinking about going to Japan and trying to get into the Eiheiji Monastery, but my spiritual adviser urged me to stay here. He said that there is nothing over there that isn't here and he was correct. I learned the truth of the Zen saying that if you are willing to travel around the world to meet a teacher, one will appear next door." (*Steve Jobs* by Walter Isaacson)

Of course, spiritual practice is by no means the sage's patent for enlightenment, nor is it the epoch-making secret of the leaders of enterprise, it is something that all ordinary people can undertake. No matter your age, gender, status, or occupation you can create a secret chamber of the spirit for yourself in your daily life whenever you like and from thence set out on the road to spiritual practice.

When Steve Jobs's spiritual adviser said "there is nothing over there that isn't here," he did not mean that the spiritual strength of the teachers of the Zen centers in America was powerful and not inferior to that in Japan. He was saying: "The practice of Zen is not somewhere else, it is in the here and now, because what you seek is something that everyone has, that does not need to be sought outside. Why then should you cross the world to look for something that you already have?"

Consequently, the creation of your own spiritual secret chamber does not require you to distance yourself

from the madding crowd and take to the hills. Whether
Sakyamuni, Jesus, Mohammed, or even Wang Yangming,
their enlightenment may have taken advantage of a period of
distance from the red dust but this distance is just a stage in
the process of spiritual practice. Its aim is not to escape the
world but, through it, to gain greater clarity of mind and to
return to purify the world with a sense of compassion.

In other words, the true spiritual secret chamber is not
a space or place apart from the world but a mental state that
transcends the commonplace. One who undertakes spiritual
practice and chooses, for a while, to turn his back on people
and society is not escaping from society or expressing hatred
of it, but rebuilding his relationship with people and society
on a different basis.

As Wang Yangming said: "The pure mind does not
abandon the ways of the world to exist in solitude."
(*Instructions for Practical Living, Vol. II*)

Marcus Aurelius, the Roman emperor and Stoic
philosopher (121–180) said: "Men seek retreats for
themselves, houses in the country, seashores, and
mountains; and thou too are wont to desire such things very
much. But this is altogether a mark of the most common
sort of men, for it is in thy power whenever thou shalt
choose to retire into thyself. For nowhere either with more
quiet or more freedom from trouble does a man retire than
into his own soul, particularly when he has within him such
thoughts that by looking into them he is immediately in
perfect tranquility; and I affirm that tranquility is nothing
else than the good ordering of the mind. Constantly then

give to thyself this retreat, and renew thyself; and let thy
principles be brief and fundamental, which, as soon as thou
shalt recur to them, will be sufficient to cleanse the soul
completely, and to send thee back free from all discontent
with the things to which thou returnest." (*Meditations*)

> I've built my hut amidst this world of men,
> Yet without the clatter of horse and cart.
> If you asked how could that be?
> I'd say I float distant from this dusty world ...

This poem by the Wei and Jin dynasties (220–420) poet
Tao Yuanming (352 or 365–427) completely accords with
the views of Marcus Aurelius described above. There is
no need at all to seek inner tranquility amongst hills and
forests. Even if you lived in the bustling "world of men" you
wouldn't hear the clatter of horse and cart. Why is this? It is
because you possess a secret chamber of the spirit remote
from the hubbub of the dusty world and your life has
naturally and gradually drawn away from the restlessness of
actuality.

> Why need the scenery of hills and water for the
>   practice of Zen?
> Quench the fires of mind,
> And you will be cool enough.
> [Record of the Jade Rock by the Song dynasty
>   Zen master Keqin (1063–1135)]

Chapter 3
Personality Is the Source of Happiness

A pupil suffered a disease of the eyes and was much distressed thereby. Master Yangming said: "You value your eyes, yet despise your mind."

Instructions for Practical Living, Vol. I, Record of Xue Kan

The majority of us are like the pupil who valued his eyes but despised his mind. We spend our life busy with worries about our body of flesh and blood, in anxiety and in activity, but rarely do we have any care for our mind or whether or not it is healthy. It is as the 20th-century American humanistic psychologist Abraham Maslow said: "For those who prefer seeing to being blind, feeling good to feeling bad, wholeness to being crippled, it can be recommended that they seek psychological health."

It is regrettable that we have only ever understood how to take care of our sight and have allowed "the eyes of our soul" to sink into darkness; we are much concerned with the wholeness of our body and with our health but disregard the crippling of our mind and the pathological changes of psychological illness.

Man lives in the world, and must first satisfy the basic requirements of existence like clothing, food, shelter, and work, of this there can be no doubt. But if someone possesses no spiritual requirements higher than these, then that is tragic. Because, apart from his body, man has both soul and spirit (generally referred to by Wang Yangming as "Mind"). If someone only knows how to value the former and despises or forgets the latter then it is the same as degrading oneself to the state of a "non-person," a low-grade animal.

Maslow divided man's requirements into a five-tier "hierarchy of needs": physiological, safety, love and belonging, esteem, and self-actualization. Self-actualization was considered to be the highest tier of the hierarchy and referred to the potential for the growth and wholeness of self. Maslow said: "A musician must make music, an artist must paint, a poet must write, if he is to be ultimately at peace with himself. What a man can be, he must be. He must be true to his own nature."

Maslow's "self-actualization" would, in Confucian terms and in the language of Wang Yangming's School of Mind, be called "being oneself" or "becoming oneself," meaning that one took responsibility upon oneself for achieving the inner quality and perfection of one's own character.

In the view of Wang Yangming, the most important thing in life was what one became and not what one possessed in terms of material goods, or how other people looked on one. The 19th-century German philosopher Schopenhauer took a similar point of view, believing that "what you are" was far more important than "what you have" or "the opinion of other people" because no matter when and where he was, a man's quality and character followed him. Consequently, the fortunes and misfortunes of life were, at the very least, because they were things that descended upon us, mainly determined by our own quality and character. He said "what you are" and "the thing innate to all man" was called character and that everything it created was the only direct source of our happiness and the rest was just means and medium that could have no particular effect on happiness.

However, people today have turned the idea on its head and pay excessive attention to the externalities of status, position, wealth, and reputation and have little regard to their own character and inner quality. If somebody has no understanding of the fact that the real self is determined by one's inner qualities, he will center his life in the external world and adopt currently fashionable social values and standards to assess and define himself, and employ the views and opinions of others to determine his lifestyle and thinking, thus sacrificing sovereignty over his whole life.

It is difficult to enjoy truly permanent happiness in this kind of life and even if one could it would be evanescent— for happiness just built on external factors is easily lost through changes in the external state.

How then does one act to take back control of one's life and secure truly long-lasting happiness?

Wang Yangming would answer: "Protect your mind."

Put in concrete terms, this is to perfect your character, create superior spiritual qualities, and to realize the possibilities for good in one's character to the greatest extent possible.

If we say that character is the source of happiness then we can also say that virtue is the strongest defender of human welfare.

There is a universal misunderstanding about virtue

that considers that the nurture of a virtuous character is a social duty and a demand of external ethics. In fact, this opinion is biased. First, virtue refers to an inner spiritual quality, it is only when it is expressed externally that it becomes the ethics of another. As we have indicated above, it is somebody's inner spiritual quality that fundamentally determines their quality of life. Hence, if somebody wishes to enjoy a life of high quality then he must possess a high level of virtue. It is in this sense that somebody who really understands his responsibilities to himself, and is devoted to improving moral qualities, will enjoy his heaven-sent privileges rather than practice the ethical obligations forced upon him by society.

People harbor a second common doubt about virtue: in real life we frequently encounter people who consistently profit from turning their backs on virtue. Equally, there are also some virtuous people who not only fail to profit from it but actually suffer loss. That being so, what grounds do we have for asserting that virtue can accomplish well-being in life? In other words, is not the saying "virtue is rewarded with virtue and evil with evil" in reality not only empty but even contrary in meaning?

Zhou Guoping, the present-day Chinese philosopher (1945–), has made a penetrating analysis of this. He believes that as far as both good and evil people are concerned, the differences in their inner spiritual quality will cause marked differences of interpretation and reaction even in similar external circumstances. For example, it is difficult for good people and evil people both, to escape the suffering of the world, but as St Augustine (354–430) once said: "The same suffering will be confirmation, baptism and purification to the virtuous man but to the evil doer it will be a curse, calamity and ruin." In the same way, a similar external blessing such as wealth may engender a mood of leisure, sufficiency, and generosity in the virtuous but become an anxiety, a halter round the neck, and a burden for the wicked. In all, therefore, both the disaster and the happiness of the secular world may be transformed into spiritual value for the virtuous but for the wicked they can be a punishment. The virtuous sow spiritual seed and reap spiritual value, this is the reward of virtue. The evildoer lives a life of wickedness without ever experiencing anything of positive spiritual value, this is the reward of evil. When your body shines with the glory of human nature and makes you feel proud, this glory and pride is your reward and you will truly feel that external events and circumstances are unimportant.

Put simply, happiness is not the reward of virtue, it is virtue itself.

Chapter 4
Knowing One's Original Self

Lu Cheng says in his letter: "The Buddhist concept of 'coming to know one's original self by thinking neither of good nor evil' is not the same as the Confucian concept of 'seeking through the examination of things.' But if I use ultimate knowledge when I am unaware of either good or evil, then I am already involved in thinking of good. If I wish to be aware of neither good nor evil and the conscience of the mind to be at peace and at ease, that can only occur at the point between sleeping and waking ... I desire to seek tranquility, however, the more there is no tranquility, the more I wish ideas should not be born but the more they are born. How can I cause this mind of mine to obliterate previous ideas and prevent the emergence of future ideas and allow conscience alone to manifest itself, so that I may roam with the creator of all thing?"

Wang Yangming's reply: "The concept of 'coming to know one's original self by thinking neither of good nor evil' was devised by the Buddhists for the convenience of those who do not yet know their original self. The original self is what Confucianists like me term conscience and now that we are fully aware of conscience there is no need for such a way of putting it. 'Seeking through the examination of things' is a function of ultimate knowledge, what the Buddhists call alertness or clarity of mind, it is also the maintenance of their original self ... Conscience is just conscience and when you come to analyze the difference between good and evil, what more good and what more evil is there to consider? The substance of conscience already derives from tranquility but now we have added to it a search for tranquility; the origins of conscience sprang from life but now we have added a desire for 'non-life,' it is not only the conscience of Confucianism that is not like this, even Buddhism is not this selfishly single minded. There is just the concept of conscience, from head to tail, with neither beginning nor end, that is to say previous ideas are not obliterated and future ideas do not occur. To desire the destruction of previous ideas and the non-occurrence of future ideas is what the Buddhists term the 'annihilation of one's nature,' just dust and ashes."

> *Instructions for Practical Living, Vol. II,*
> *Answer to Lu Cheng's Letter about Tranquility*

The second volume of *Instructions for Practical Living* is a compilation of Wang Yangming's correspondence with his disciples. The two passages above are the contents of an exchange of letters with his disciple Lu Cheng.

Lu Cheng, styled Yuanjing, was a native of Wuxing in Zhejiang Province. In his letter he raised a well-known Zen topic: "When thinking neither of good nor evil what is the original state of your intelligence?" Meaning, what is your true self?

If it were you, how would you approach this topic? In all your life, have you ever thought of going in search of your true self?

Some successful people may laugh at this question: why should I go in search of my true self? Do you mean to say that I am someone who is not their true self? I am Tom of Tom, Dick, and Harry, I am a successful entrepreneur, I have a virtuous, good-looking wife, three clever children, a job I love, and a collection of interesting and congenial friends … with a life as good as this, why should I go looking for some "true self"?

If that is your answer, then I must congratulate you, for you have all that a man could desire. However, Mr. Tom, I would like to ask you: "Can you put an 'equals' sign between 'Tom' and the 'things' that you own?" You say that you are Tom, but Tom is just a symbol. You might just as well be called Dick or Harry but whatever name you have, it cannot eradicate your true self. Thus, we can see that it is inaccurate to say "you are Tom." Rather, we should say "you are called Tom."

For the same reason, we cannot say "you are a successful entrepreneur" because entrepreneur is just your position and not yourself. The day you change occupations and become a politician or go into academia and become a professor, you are not going to change into somebody else. So, we cannot say "you are a successful entrepreneur" but should say "you have the status of entrepreneur."

Let's take another look. Your wife and children, your occupation and friends, like your name and status, are all social relationships or things that you own but they are not you. In other words, what you "are" and what you "have" are two completely different things and cannot be confused.

You might reply, "Even if you are right and none of this is my true self, however, I'm just under six-foot tall, in good health, handsome, articulate, well informed with wide interests … are these inherent characteristics?"

Sorry, Mr. Tom, I regret to say that, of course, these are of you but they are not inherently you. Illness and calamity (including elective plastic surgery and gender change) may alter your external characteristics and physical condition, so "just under six-foot tall, in good health, handsome" are not innate characteristics; moreover, the brain may also be affected by illness and calamity and suffer memory loss, so "articulate, well informed with wide interests" are not inherent characteristics either.

In sum, therefore, the "self" that is normally recognized by the vast majority of people as being comprised of name, gender, occupation, status, economic condition, personal relationships, physical characteristics, nature, memory, feelings, knowledge, mood, aspirations, and ideological outlook is actually not the real "self" but a false self, a combination of causes, what the Buddhists call a "synergy of conditions."

This synergy of conditions refers to all the various things that, under certain circumstances, come together in combination. The false self is not to say that the self of the synergy of conditions does not exist, but that were the circumstances to alter then the self would alter with them and is therefore not permanent.

Given that the things described above are merely a false self, what is the real self?

In fact, the true self is not outside the false self but inside it.

If you identify with everything that is internal and external to body and mind, your true self will be lost within the false self; it is only when you no longer identify with anything that you possess that your false self can be completely transformed into your true self. To take an analogy: the true self is an actor and the false self the character that he plays. The actor must internalize the role and become the character that he plays but he must also externalize and always remember that he is acting. It is only when he has grasped the fact that this is the appropriate way of performing that he can be described as an outstanding actor. If an actor submerges too deeply in his character and believes the artificiality of the plot to be reality, then he loses both his true self and his ability to be master of it.

Consequently, identifying with the false self is tantamount to handing yourself over to director Fate, so that when fate creates circumstances in which you weep, then you weep and when it creates different circumstances in which you laugh, then you laugh. However, somebody who identifies with the true self may under the same director similarly encounter all manner of situations both tragic and happy but, like the best actors, he will in the course of expressing grief and anger, sorrow and joy, keep clearly in mind the fact that this is just part of the drama of life and that his role is to play his own part and to experience all that is in the play, but without needing to immerse himself so deeply in the part that he cannot extricate himself.

Put simply, people who know their true self are "acting" and can take control at any time; but those who identify with the false self are in the position of "the play acting me" and can only remain in the red dust in a state of confusion, driven hither and thither by the waves and currents of life.

To know with clarity that one is "acting" is the "conscience" of Wang Yangming; to know with clarity who you are and not to identify with the theatrical character is the knowledge of the original self of Zen.

Wang Yangming believed that these two were actually the same: "The original self is what Confucianists like me term conscience."

It was because of this correspondence between the concepts of conscience and original self that Lu Cheng undertook his examination of the Sixth Zen Patriarch Huineng's point about "Thinking neither of Virtue nor Evil." However, Lu Cheng misunderstood the true implication of Huineng's statement and erroneously interpreted it as "In leisured calm no thought will arise," an idea totally at odds with Huineng's original meaning.

The reason that Huineng proposed the theory above was in no way to put us on the path towards the concept of "In leisured calm no thought will arise" but to cause us to overthrow the inertial thinking of the theory of opposites, or as Maslow put it: "The elimination of dichotomy."

Maslow believed that a common characteristic of the subjects of self-actualization that he studied was the elimination of "if not this then that." He said: "Like the greatest artists they were able to take mutually clashing colors, shapes, and uncoordinated bits and pieces and assemble them into a united whole. This is what the greatest theoreticians do when they assemble puzzling and disconnected fragments into a complete whole. The greatest politicians, religious leaders, philosophers, mothers and fathers, lovers and inventors, are all the same. They are synthesizers who can integrate unassociated and even contradictory things into a single whole."

If we can dispense with our sense of distinctions and incorporate contradictory elements into a united whole, then there will be no need to cut off the flow of thought from the mind, and all that will be required will be the maintenance of the capacity for penetrating analysis and enlightened examination of all the phenomena that are both internal and external to body and mind.

Regrettably, Lu Cheng was unable to understand this point. On the one hand he examined Huineng's pronouncement but on the other became entangled with the concepts of the good and evil of phenomena and the birth and destruction of ideas. In this way, Zen was not only unable to help him throw off his burdens, it could only cause him to descend into deeper confusion.

Then, how can we come to any profound understanding of the state of "thinking of neither good nor evil"? Have there been times in our own lives when we have been in this state?

The answer is "yes," when we were at the beginning of life, that is, when identification with the false self had not yet taken place.

The beginning of life? The state of infancy? It is indeed, the state of infancy.

We have all been infants, an existence without anxieties, worries, competition, pressure, distinctions, and attachments. When we were hungry, we bawled for our mother's breast; when we were full, we slept sweetly. In our eyes, everything in this world was fresh and good, everything that came into our hands was a toy to be played with. We were full of vitality and we possessed a joy and a sufficiency that came with life and did not need to be sought elsewhere. We were at one with the world, everything was perfect, plentiful, and pure. So far as we were concerned, "existence" was a magnificent gift bestowed upon us by heaven; "living" for us, was the utter blessing of the creator.

In short, the state of infancy was lived entirely in the present.

Thereafter, as we gradually grew up and developed an awareness of the distinction of opposites, we created a rift between us and existence, gradually plunging into a great chasm. We began to separate mine and yours, good and bad, beautiful and ugly, right and wrong, advantage and disadvantage, like and loathing ...

Later, we were left with love and hate and suffering and joy and pursuit and escape and possession and competition and anxiety and worry and loathing and fear and ...

Thus, in our eyes, the original perfect world split into a world of countless binary opposites. Our life became a series of unending contradictions, disputes, clashes, and games with self, others, the environment, and society, to the weariness of the spirit and exhaustion of strength, to chronic illness, to old age, and to death itself.

When our mind turned from sufficiency to deficiency, our life was then no longer a gift but a punishment; when we split a limitless and perfect existence into so many fragments, living turned from a blessing to a curse.

What should we do?

The Buddha said: let go the mind of distinctions and attachments, see your original mind.

Laozi said: to know male and to know female, return to infancy.

Mengzi said: on the road to maturity do not forget the mind of a child.

Of course, the statements "return to infancy" and "do

not forget the mind of a child" do not compel us to reduce the level of our intelligence to that of a child, nor do they incite us to abandon civilized society to lead a savage and primitive life in the hills. They encourage us, like children and infants, to live perfectly in the present, filled with the joy of existence and enjoying the intrinsic purity, perfection, and richness of life and to glow with vitality and creativity.

In the words of Maslow, this was called "Second Naivete" and was one of the most important characteristics of self-actualization. Maslow believed: "The creativeness of the self-actualized man seems rather to be kin to the naïve and universal creativeness of unspoiled children. It seems to be more a fundamental characteristic of common human nature—a potentiality given to all human beings at birth."

We can see that resuming the childlike mind is not a simple matter of reversing cognitive strength or physiological withdrawal to an original state, but a denial of denial, a cyclical ascent, an ordinariness of total glory, and a phoenix-like rebirth in Nirvana.

The Tang dynasty Zen Master Qingyuan Weixin once described the three stages of his own lifetime engagement with Zen:

> "Thirty years ago, before I had been engaged with Zen, I saw a mountain as a mountain and water as water. Later, when I had attained the virtue of knowledge and had achieved an entry through the senses, I saw that mountains were not mountains and that water was not water. Now that I have achieved

a state of joy without attachments and distinctions,
I see that mountains are just mountains and water is
just water."

When we reach the third stage we see the scenery
of the original landscape with absolute clarity. Despite
seeing that mountains are still mountains and that water is
still water, everything external seems not to have changed
at all when compared with the first stage. In fact, it is
completely different, because our inner mind has undergone
a fundamental change, as if the gradually increasing light
of perception has, in the space of a moment, suddenly
illuminated everything within and without both body and mind.

The modern Vietnamese Zen Master Thich Nhat Hanh
has said: "In the same way as the sun of the natural world
shines upon every leaf and blade of grass, our enlightened
consciousness should take care of our every thought and
feeling so that we may change them and understand their
birth, retention, and destruction. We should not judge or
criticize them nor should we pander to them or destroy
them … Do not turn your spirit into a battlefield, there
is no need for warfare there because your feelings of joy,
sorrow, anger, and hatred are part of you … Enlightened
consciousness is a lenient and well-ordered state, it is
without violence and makes no distinctions. Its objective is
to discern and understand thinking and emotion and not to
make judgements about virtue and evil, good and bad, or to
place them in opposing camps, thus causing mutual conflict.
People often describe the hostility between virtue and evil

as being analogous to light and dark, but if we look at it from another angle, we will discover that when light appears darkness disappears. Darkness has not gone but has been absorbed by the light and has become light."

Master Thich Nhat Hanh's statement corroborates Wang Yangming's remark that: "If man can know the secret of conscience, then all his evil thoughts and mad ideas will, at a stroke, melt away; truly the heart contains a grain of purity that can turn all to gold." (*Instructions for Practical Living, Vol. III*)

The day that light appears, darkness will be absorbed into light.

This is the wisdom of Zen, and also the wisdom of the School of Mind.

In fact, this wisdom is not just the wisdom of Zen or of the School of Mind. According to modern psychology, the power of intense feelings and violent notions will quickly dissipate or change if we are able to consider them coolly. It was in this sense that Wang Yangming was able to tell Lu Cheng that conscience was just conscience and that when one came to analyze the difference between good and evil, what more good and what more evil was there to consider? The essence of the practice of self-cultivation was not to turn one's mind into a battlefield. There was no need either to pander to or reject ideas, concepts, moods, feelings, or thoughts, or to separate from one's attachment to them. One was only required to use one's conscience to illuminate all with enlightenment.

In fact, the true self has never departed, it has been there all the time, it is just that we were not aware of it.

Chapter 5
Retrieving the Joy of Mind

*Lu Cheng says in a letter:"The Song dynasty philosopher of the
School of Reason, Zhou Dunyi, often asked his pupil Cheng Hao
to seek out the joy of Confucius and his pupil Yan Hui. May I
dare ask whether this joy is the same or not as the joy of the seven
emotions? If it is the same then all that the ordinary person could
desire may be enjoyed, and why therefore need sages? But if there is
another true joy, then, when a sage encounters sorrow, anger, alarm,
and fear does this true joy still exist or not? Moreover, the mind of
a gentleman is often of cautious fear, this is a lifelong anxiety, how
may one obtain joy? I am normally depressed and have never seen
true joy and would dearly wish to seek it."*

*Master Yangming replied:"Joy is of the original essence of
substance of the mind and though it is not the same as the joy
of the seven emotions it is not outside them. Although sages have
another true joy, it is also similarly possessed by the ordinary person
who does not know that he possesses it and in seeking it brings
much suffering upon himself and amidst confusion loses it. Though
he may be lost in suffering and confusion and ever without the joy,
the moment there is enlightenment of thought and he returns to
sincerity, then it is there. In discussion with you it is never other
than this meaning. For you to persist in asking 'what path should I
take' is rather like searching for a donkey when riding one."*

Instructions for Practical Living, Vol. II, Reply to Lu Cheng

In this letter Lu Cheng raised the subject of happiness, a
universal concern.

Everybody lives in the world but they do not all want the same thing. Some like power, yet others feel that it is more relaxing to be an ordinary person; some like money yet others feel instead that too much money is a disaster; some like beauty but others believe that sex is as dangerous as a knife; some like the company of friends, others like peace and solitude; some like to travel the world, others believe the world of the mind to be vaster. Nevertheless, if you asked everybody if they wished for happiness, the answer would be a unanimous "yes."

Everybody aspires to happiness. Psychological research indicates that when we are happy our thought processes are more active, our general performance more remarkable, our body more healthy, and even our physiological functions more effective. Relevant psychological experiments demonstrate that when we are in a happy frame of mind our sight, taste, hearing, and sense of smell are all more sensitive and that when we come into contact with other people or objects they sense more subtle changes. Psychosomatic medicine has confirmed that in a state of happiness, the heart, liver, stomach, and other internal organs all function better than normal. Consequently, there are a number of Western doctors who have announced that unhappiness is the root of all disease and that happiness is the only medicine.

Setting aside, for the moment, the question of whether or not these conclusions are excessively arbitrary, we must accept, at the very least, that happiness is something good and something that everybody wishes for. But, what is it and how do we achieve it? Is the happiness of the ordinary person and the happiness of the School of Mind one and the same thing?

This was precisely Lu Cheng's question. In his letter to Wang Yangming he raised the concept of "the happiness of Confucius and Yan Hui." This is a reference to the spirit of finding peace in poverty and joy in the Way and is a quotation from the *Analects*, where Confucius says in praise of his disciple Yan Hui: "Worthy indeed is Yan Hui! A bowl of rice, a ladle of water, living humbly in an alley, none could bear this hardship but Yan Hui is happy in it and does not change." How is it that Yan Hui can be happy in a situation that the ordinary person would find intolerable?

In fact, the answer is very simple: Yan Hui's happiness derives from a maturity of mind and perfection of character that is based upon the perfection and sufficiency of his inner world. Hence, happiness is his constant companion. By contrast, the happiness of the man in the world is always driven by material aspiration and derives from an inner deficiency. It must be in ceaseless external pursuit before it can fill the cavities of his inner mind and he can enjoy a moment of pleasure.

People frantically seek happiness externally, sometime they achieve it and sometimes not. Admittedly there can be suffering in failing to achieve it, but even if achieved it is hard for it to be permanent and one can only seek fresh prey and hope that it will bring true happiness, but the result is always the same.

It is not difficult to arrive at a conclusion from all the

above: to obtain long-lasting happiness through the possession of more and more external objects is to move entirely in the wrong direction. The single-minded pursuit of things that resemble happiness will always be a source of trouble.

There are a number of important points in Wang Yangming's answer to Lu Cheng's question:

The happiness of sages is not the same as that of ordinary people.

The happiness of sages is the happiness of maturity of mind and perfection of character, as the 17th-century Dutch philosopher Spinoza said: "Happiness is not the reward of virtue, but is virtue itself." This kind of virtue proceeds from within to without and emerges naturally. It is sufficient to itself and fundamentally does not require any external support. Consequently, Wang Yangming called it "true joy." However, the happiness of the ordinary person is mainly based upon external objects that have to be acquired. Happiness is only felt after desires have been satisfied, thus, the two are not the same.

Despite the fact that the happiness of sages is not the same as that of ordinary people, nevertheless, it does not stand outside that of ordinary people.

Whilst this statement may sound obscure, its meaning is quite simple: the happiness of sages is not something remote and unfamiliar, vague or empty but something that can be experienced by ordinary people once trained in the School of Mind. In other words, although the happiness of the sages is not the same as the happiness of ordinary people, it is very definitely the happiness of the ordinary mind.

Because of this, Wang Yangming immediately makes the following point:

Originally, ordinary people also possessed the happiness of the sages. Unfortunately, it was mislaid, but it was not lost.

The logic employed here by Wang Yangming has been consistent, a patient and painstaking reminder to all of us that we are indeed fundamentally perfect and sufficient, so why do we "always throw away our own inexhaustible household treasure and take an alms bowl to beg from door to door"? The Heavenly Principle is within us, what is it that we seek without? Conscience is in our mind, what are we looking for outside? True happiness is of the mind, spending each and every day in a troublesome external search for happiness, is that not to seek vexation for oneself and to crave the taste of bitterness?

Once there is a moment of enlightened thought and a return to sincerity happiness may be found. There will be no need to seek a donkey while riding upon one.

If we only adjust the direction of travel of a mind accustomed to the pursuit of material desire and construct the meaning of life around the growth and perfection of the mind, thus allowing us to face our inner mind with sincerity, uninfluenced by external values or the views of others and untroubled by our own desires or state of mind, then utter happiness will spring forth from within our own mind.

Of course, the emphasis of Wang Yangming's School of

Mind upon the happiness derived from the growth of the mind and the perfection of character does not mean to say that we cannot enjoy the material happiness of the ordinary world at the same time. There is no contradiction between the two, indeed they complement each other: the healthier the mind and character, the more permanent the happiness derived from life and the less it is a by-product.

Following on from this, Lu Cheng's question is: "When a sage encounters situations of anxiety, anger, alarm, and fear, does his happiness still exist?"

In truth, the answer to this already lies within his question. Lu Cheng asked whether, when a sage "encountered situations" of anxiety, anger, alarm, and fear, he was still happy or not, not whether when a sage "produced a mood" of anxiety, anger, alarm, and fear, he was still happy or not. Putting aside the question of happy or not for the moment, let us examine the distinction between these two formulations: the first refers to encountering a bad situation, and the second to the emergence of a mood. Thus, we can see that encountering a situation and the emergence of a mood are not the same thing at all. In other words, when someone encounters a situation that may cause him anxiety, anger, alarm, or fear it may not necessarily produce a mood of anxiety, anger, alarm, or fear at all.

Relevant psychological research indicates that there are two major causes of unhappiness: our tendency to assume that things that basically have nothing to do with us are in fact aimed at us; and our subconscious desire to bring the uncontrollable under control.

Unhappiness is a habit and so is happiness. Happiness is purely a matter of the inner mind—and the things that cause us unhappiness are not external, they are our beliefs, our ideas, and our attitudes, that is to say our own mind. Conversely, happiness is the same. Consequently, if we can alter our defensive tendency and abandon our desire to control the external world, we can then throw off its control of us and retrieve that happiness that was originally ours.

Thus, Lu Cheng's question answers itself. When sages encounter these emotions they normally ask themselves: why do I allow external factors to determine my mood, responses, and behavior? Subsequently they are able to brush them aside and to float away—this is the sage who, like Yan Hui, can exist on "a bowl of rice, a ladle of water," while the other may "sit and watch the courtyard flowers blossom and fall, the clouds in the heavens furl and unfurl." At this point who can doubt the existence of their happiness?

In fact, one of the major functions/achievements of the School of Mind is to nurture the habit of happiness to the point where self becomes the source of happiness. In Wang Yangming's words: "Constant happiness is an achievement." (*Instructions for Practical Living, Vol. III*)

Lu Cheng's final question is: "The mind of the gentleman must always be in a state of cautious fear, this is lifelong suffering, how can he be happy?"

This question springs from a misinterpretation of "cautious fear"—that assumes that this indicates a permanent state of heightened anxiety. In fact, the meaning is that in order to avoid fault, a man of virtue and refinement must be vigilant and self-controlled in situations unobserved by others and maintain his self-respect in situations that may not be overheard by others.

Thus, as we have discussed before, the fundamental meaning of "must always be in a state of cautious fear" is awareness and enlightened consciousness. In Wang Yangming's own words: "Prudent fear is the achievement of conscience. The scholar constantly observes that which cannot be seen and constantly listens to that which cannot be heard before achievement can be established. After it has matured over time, then it requires neither effort nor inspection and true character may continue as itself without end." (*Instructions for Practical Living, Vol. III*)

Wang Yangming always believed that the function or achievement of this kind of conscience was active. Not only did it have no relationship at all with heightened anxiety, it was one of the greatest joys: "If one can gain it (conscience) complete with the least defect, then one may dance for joy. I do not know what other happiness there may be between heaven and earth that may replace it." (*Instructions for Practical Living, Vol. III*)

In this atmosphere, how can such self-possessed freedom, such cheerful independence, be called "lifelong suffering." How can it stand opposed to happiness?

Part III

The Unity of Knowledge and Action: Knowledge Is the Beginning of Action and Action Is the Culmination of Knowledge

For Zhu Xi, there were two worlds, the abstract world of Reason and the concrete physical world. For Wang Yangming, however, there was only one, the world upon which he had bestowed meaning. That is to say, neither the world of Reason nor the material world could generate meaning unless empowered by the projections and conceptual systems of the subjective awareness of the self. Consequently, knowledge was the search for and establishment of meaning (knowledge is the beginning of action), in itself a kind of action; while action was the revelation and completion of meaning (action is the culmination of knowledge), and was thus inseparable from knowledge. When Wang Yangming refers to "knowledge" and "action" he is referring to the developmental process of constructing this kind of world of meaning. Knowledge is the construction of a set of views on the world, on life and on values that are consistent with the Way of the sages; action is the implementation and deepening of one's cognition and conceptualization through interaction with other people and with the external world and others.

Chapter 6
Constructing One's Own World of Meaning

Knowledge is the aim of action and action is the implementation of knowledge; knowledge is the beginning of action and action is the outcome of knowledge. If one were to understand and speak of knowledge only, then action already exists within it; to speak solely of action, then knowledge already exists within it. The ancients who spoke first of "knowledge" and then later of "action" did so because people were of one kind only, acting randomly in confusion, completely without understanding of thought or self-examination, and behaving out of blind ignorance and hence speaking first of knowledge and only then separately of action. There is yet another kind of person, who thinks in a void, unwilling to personally engage, merely groping for effect, who hence speaks of action first before knowledge can attain truth. This is the speech of ancients obliged to remedy past error. Were they able to see the true meaning, a single word would have been enough. Nevertheless, people today divide action from knowledge believing that one must first know before being able to act. Were I, today, to propound and debate and spend effort upon knowledge and wait upon it for truth and only then devote time to action, there would be no action in a lifetime, and no knowledge either. This is not the minor illness of a day. Now, when I speak of the unity of knowledge and action, that is really the cure for this illness, it is no empty fabrication of mine. The original

substance of knowledge and action was ever thus.
Instructions for Practical living, Vol. I, Record of Xu Ai

"The unity of knowledge and action" is a core proposition
of Wang Yangming's School of Mind. As commonly
understood, "knowledge" refers to learning and cognition,
"action" refers to practice and operation. Man must
necessarily be aware of things and study them before
being able to practice and operate in life. At this juncture,
knowledge and action appear as two distinctly different
things. However, why did Wang Yangming speak of "the unity
of knowledge and action"? Did he want to combine the two
things into a single entity?

No, Wang Yangming's true intention was to propose
that knowledge and action had originally been a single
entity, at least in a Confucian context, and were indivisible.

"There is but a single competence to the learning of the
sages, knowledge and action are indivisible." (*Instructions for
Practical Living, Vol. I*)

Wang Yangming believed this because he considered
that in this context "knowledge" was not absolutely confined
to an awareness of things. More importantly, it was an
awareness of self, a realization of the "original substance of
mind." In the language of today, "primal awareness."

Of a necessity, primal awareness involves our whole
conceptual system, that is, our world outlook, our outlook
on life and our system of values. One has only to mention
the word "knowledge" in the context of the School of Mind
and it raises the following questions: How do we regard the

world? What is the origin of the world? What is more basic and more important, the spiritual or the material? What does man live for? What is the fundamental meaning of life? What is it that we should seek? How are we to determine right and wrong, virtue and evil, good and bad, correct and incorrect? Is morality an integral component of life or a later acquisition? Should we practice morality in life? And so on.

Man is the product of conceptions. Man chooses and builds a certain kind of conceptual system and then becomes that kind of man and lives that kind of life.

In this sense, "choosing" and "building" are both a kind of action. The process of establishing one's own conceptual system is a form of action, whether it derives from a multitude of judgements and choices or from a complete blank. It is just that the action occurs in one's inner world and is not easily visible to outsiders.

Whether he is aware of it or not, when somebody performs an action in the external world, it is always on the basis of his own particular conceptual system. While the action may take place externally, it is rooted in the mind, it cannot be anything different, it can only be an externalization of the conceptual system.

This is why Wang Yangming says: "If one were to speak of knowledge only, then action already exists within it; to speak solely of action, then knowledge already exists within it."

When we build our own system of values it means that we are constructing a world of meaning that differs from that of other people.

In this respect, "knowledge" is basically an action
undertaken in the building of a world of meaning, so
that exercising the mind and mobilizing thought are both
actions. "When I speak of the unity of knowledge and
action, I want people to understand that setting thought
in train is an action." (*Instructions for Practical Living, Vol. III*).
Hence, action itself is the implementation and exhibition
of concept, so this kind of "action" equates to a natural
emanation of "knowledge."

In simple terms, we could say that knowledge is inner
action and that action is the externalization of concept.
They may appear different but they are the same in the
way that one may become two and two become one. Thus,
in the context of Wang Yangming's School of Mind, it is
fundamentally impossible to find knowledge without action
or action without concept.

This the basic nature of knowledge and action and the
true meaning of the unity of knowledge and action.

Of course, when Wang Yangming says that action is the
exercise of mind and the mobilization of thought, it does
not mean that these are the only functions of action. If you
have not developed conceptually through interaction with
the outside world and with other people it means that your
world of meaning has yet to be established. As a result,
this kind of "knowledge" is what Wang Yangming described
as "behaving out of blind ignorance." Moreover, if you do
not act through the unique meaning bestowed on your

world and existence by your own positive construction of a conceptual system, your actions will be blind, determined by the outside world, and incapable of being mastered by yourself, what Wang Yangming termed "acting randomly in confusion."

Thus, there are two completely different approaches to the attainment of a conceptual system: first, to accept the gifts of the external world without exercising any choice in the matter and without self-reflection; second, to consciously take the initiative in seeking out and building such a system.

Everybody, no matter whether they are aware or not, is cognizant of the world on the basis of a specific worldview, a view of life and values, and acts on their basis. For most of us, our conceptual system is fundamentally built during the process of growing up and is bestowed and inculcated by the imperceptible influences of family, school, and society. In this way, although it is a "world of meaning" that has been interpreted and determined, it is, nevertheless, one tossed in by external forces and your freedom and initiative have been disengaged in advance.

There are a few people who do not totally accept the conceptual system bestowed by the external world and build a system for themselves based on reasonable doubt and independent thought, much like that displayed during the knowledge-seeking period of Wang Yangming's youth. Consequently, as you search, in bewilderment and hope, for the "world of meaning" that belongs to you, you are already exercising initiative and independence and your "basic inner nature" is quietly taking shape. All the possibilities for good in human nature are opening up for you. It is because your "world of meaning" is not a given one but derives from initiative and search and is self-built, that the strength and wisdom that you obtain in the process, and the meaning and values created in the end, cannot be matched by any preceding system.

The "knowledge" and "action" of Wang Yangming refer to the process of developing this kind of world of meaning. "Knowledge" refers to the establishment of a worldview, a view of life and values that are consistent with the Way of the sages. "Action" refers to the establishment and deepening of one's awareness and concepts through interaction with the external world and other people. In actual fact, the two are descriptions of the same thing seen from two different angles.

For Zhu Xi, there were two worlds, the abstract world of Reason or Principle and the concrete physical world; but for Wang Yangming there was only the one to which he had assigned meaning. That is to say, both the physical and abstract worlds had to be empowered by the projections and conceptual systems of the subjective awareness of the self before they could generate meaning. Thus, in Wang Yangming's School of Mind, knowledge was the search for and establishment of meaning (knowledge is the beginning of action), in itself a kind of action; whilst action was the development and perfection of meaning (action is the culmination of knowledge) and thus cannot be separated from knowledge.

In Wang Yangming's School of Mind, knowledge and action present as an indivisible whole, thus, the world of meaning constructed from the unity of knowledge and action is also blended into a complete whole, with no difference between inside and outside or mind and matter, or between a part and the whole. Consequently, Wang Yangming is able to say: "A part of knowledge is the whole of knowledge, the whole of knowledge is a part of knowledge." (*Instructions for Practical Living, Vol. III*)

Wang Yangming's statement looks to be a denial of general knowledge, as if the parts and whole of something can contain each other—it is easy to understand how the whole may contain a part but how is it possible to understand how a part may contain the whole?

The modern scientific technique of holography is one in which the whole and part may each contain each other. For example, if a hologram is a picture of a face, and you tear it up and then pick up one of the tiny pieces at random and enlarge it, it will still be a complete face. Any microscopic piece of a hologram will contain all the information of the whole, whatever object is photographed holographically, hence the name "hologram." This is to say that in a hologram, not only does the whole contain a part but the part also contains the whole.

Seen this way, Wang Yangming's statement is easy to understand. His objection to the division of knowledge and action into two and emphasis on the non-existence of any difference between whole and part was in the hope that through the unity of knowledge and action of the School of Mind we would construct a "hologrammatic" world of meaning. It was only in this way that we could infuse our work and daily life with a complete and creative strength and invest our most trivial acts, our dealings with others, our comings and goings, and our quiet moments with a transcendent and divine meaning.

Maslow once advanced a proposition of "Being cognition (B-cognition)" that was very much in tune with the "unity of knowledge and action" of Wang Yangming's School of Mind. "Being cognition" is a new kind of cognitive ability acquired during the process of self-actualization. Maslow believed that this was an innate understanding. He described it thus: "When awareness is at its fiercest and most absorbed, the object of its attention may be held in its entirety; at the same time, the essence of self becomes even more complete in its fusion with the object. This is a kind of dialectical and integrated awareness, an awareness that is truly spontaneous, independent and creative."

As Maslow saw it, "Being cognition" was a supra-normal understanding achieved through a "Peak-Experience" (rather like Wang Yangming's enlightenment at Longchang). At the same time, it was also a comprehension of the existing world of the noumenon. It was a highly harmonized unification of the subjective and the objective and a subtle combination of epistemology and ontology. In his original words: "In 'Being cognition,' the twins of 'what' and 'should' become one with neither difference nor contradiction. What you feel it is, is at the same time what it should be."

"What" refers to your potential, all the possibilities for good in your nature; "should" refers to the fact that when you discover your own latent potential nature, you should realize it completely, in the way that acorns "urgently require" to grow into oak trees.

"What" is an awareness of one's original nature; "should" is the action taken in order to realize one's inner nature and the two become organically combined in "existential awareness" (the unity of knowledge and action). Consequently, as long as you understand what Wang Yangming's unity of knowledge and action is, then you are on the road to Maslow's "self-actualization."

Chapter 7
Work Is Self-Cultivation

There was a subordinate judicial official, who, because he had long heard the master expound his learning, said: "This learning is excellent, but because of my burden of cases, I cannot study."

The master asked: "In what way have I told you to abandon your cases and to study in a void? Since you have court cases, then learn from them, that would be a true 'investigation of things.' In hearing a lawsuit, you do not become angry because of ill manners; nor pleased because of emollient language; nor punish an intercession; or skew one's intentions because of pleading; or deliver a careless judgement because of the complication of one's own affairs; or handle a case to accord with slanderous accusations. All these arise out of personal considerations. You must know yourself, and must look into yourself and overcome them, lest there should be the least bias that could twist right and wrong. This is the investigation that leads to knowledge. Studying whilst loaded down with cases is true study. To study whilst apart from objects and affairs is to grasp at thin air.

Instructions for Practical Living, Vol. III,
Record of Chen Jiuchuan

Man cannot live apart from society, hence self-cultivation cannot be perfected amongst hills and forests.

The story is told of an ascetic Daoist who intended to leave his village to go into the mountains to live as a hermit and practice self-cultivation, taking with him just a single piece of cloth for clothing. Washing his clothes one day up in the mountains he discovered that he needed another piece of cloth to replace the one he was washing. So, he went down the mountain and begged a piece of cloth from the villagers. The villagers, knowing him to be a devout Daoist, generously gave him a piece of cloth.

The Daoist went back up the mountain and continued to practice self-cultivation. One day he discovered by chance that there was a mouse in his hut that chewed at the spare piece of cloth as he was concentrating on meditation. Out of respect for the commandment against taking life he didn't kill the mouse but, unable to get rid of it, went down to the village again and asked the villagers for a cat.

The cat naturally frightened the mouse away. However, after a few days the Daoist discovered yet another problem: what could the cat eat? He didn't want the cat to eat mice but could he just let it eat wild herbs as he did?

So, he went down the mountain again and asked the villagers for a cow, in this way the cat could live on milk. In a little while the Daoist found out that he had to spend much time each day herding the cow, milking it, and generally looking after it to the point where it was impossible to meditate. So, he descended the mountain and found a tramp to look after the cow for him.

Having lived in the mountains for several months, the tramp began to complain that the mountains were boring, he was a normal person and he needed a wife. The Daoist thought he had a point; it was not possible to force somebody to lead an ascetic life and so had to let him find a wife. The tramp set up home, began to raise a family and his wife kept many cattle and soon there was the bustle of people. Thereupon, many people gradually moved up into the mountains and became their neighbors. Within a few short years, the Daoist was astonished and helpless to find that his hut was now surrounded by a busy village.

This story tells us that as long as one lives it is impossible to break away from people or from society.

This being the case, leaving real life in order to spend time in meditation and the investigation of things is as much nonsense as trying to fly off the ground by pulling up one's own hair.

Thus, in the view of Wang Yangming, work was the best kind of self-cultivation. "Thus, every time of day, each exchange of pleasantries, in their thousands upon thousands, are all part of the start of the flow of conscience and if you

disposed of them there would be no other conscience to
speak of." (*Instructions for Practical Living, Vol. II*)

As far as the true practitioners of the School of Mind
are concerned, none of the many strands of the experiences
of daily life, of what they say and what they do, is without a
function in the exercise of conscience. Without them there
would be no other conscience to practice.

The idea of regarding day-to-day work as self-cultivation
was not confined to Wang Yangming alone. In fact, we
can see that in Buddhism and Christianity daily labor and
mundane work can both be invested with a divine and
transcendental significance.

Zen is the model of the secular practice of Mahayana
Buddhism. The sayings of the Zen masters of the past, such
as: "The Way is our ordinary mind," "The wonders of the
Way lie in drawing water and hewing wood," "Buddhism in
the world is inseparable from an awareness of the world,"
have all raised ordinary life and daily labor to a high level of
self-cultivation.

D. T. Suzuki, the great Japanese master of Zen, said:
"The great Chinese contribution to Buddhism has been
their attitude to work. The first to employ the strength of
consciousness to make work an integral part of Buddhism
was Master Huaihai of Baizhang who lived about 1,000
years ago and was the progenitor of the move to bring the
system in Buddhist monasteries into line with that of other
Buddhist establishments." "Work was one of the monastery
rules: every monk including the masters, was required to

undertake humble physical labor, no matter how dirty it was or however much they were unwilling."

Master Huaihai of Baizhang (ca. 720–814), was a well-known Zen Master of the mid-Tang dynasty and a revolutionary figure in the history of Zen Buddhism. His greatest contribution was to overturn the traditional custom that Buddhism did not engage in production and, by a revolution in monastic system and rule, to make labor in production part of the meaning of self-cultivation. He introduced new rules that stipulated that in the monastic body there should be no division into young and old and that all should undertake productive labor. He paid no attention to his own age, led by example, and practiced what he preached.

A Song dynasty history of Zen Buddhism, the *Compendium of Five Lamps*, recorded the following story about Master Huaihai:

> The Master always took the lead in the performance of work and the undertaking of labor. The monk in charge found this unbearable, hid away the tools, and invited him to rest. The Master said: "I lack virtue, how may I ask others to labor for me?" Thereupon he searched for the tools but did not find them and thus was unwilling to eat. Hence the saying: "A day without work is a day without food" that has spread throughout the world.

The phrase "a day without work is a day without

food" demonstrates the reverent attitude of religious self-cultivation with which the Zen masters regarded the act of labor in the mundane world. The historian Yu Yingshi (1930–) said of this: "This is to fulfil one's role on earth in a transcendental and solemn spirit."

During the process of modernization in Japan, together with China, a member of the "Asian cultural circle," effort was put into the creative transformation of the spiritual traditions of Buddhism and Confucianism. The core of this transformation of tradition was the elevation of the status of ordinary work to a religious belief or a form of self-cultivation. Suzuki Shōsan (1579–1655), the well-known Tokugawa-period monk, believed that Buddhist self-cultivation was not confined to prayer and repentance but was also present in the unremitting concentration of heart and mind on the performance of labor. He was an energetic advocate of "self-cultivation in the mundane world," "self-cultivation through labor," and "occupational self-cultivation," meaning that the professional classes should put their heart into politics and administration, peasants should devote themselves to agriculture, workers should strive in manual labor, and merchants should exercise their duty in commerce. The Edo-period Confucians Ishida Baigan (1685–1744), Ninomiya Sontoku (1787–1856), and others also combined the spirit of Confucianism with the commercial thinking of the Japanese *chōnin* (tradesman or merchant) and promoted a life of diligence, frugality, and respect for duty, advocating the idea that for people to do their utmost in their occupation, working hard with respect for their calling was a mark of the worship of heaven and of moral perfection.

In his book *A Rule for Life*, the Japanese philosopher, industrialist, and loyal disciple of Wang Yangming's School of Mind, Inamori Kazuo (1932–), described the relationship between work and self-cultivation and strongly emphasized the value and significance of work and physical labor to life. He said:

> "It is generally held that reward is the aim of labor and that labor is just a means of earning a living, the happy life is one of little work, much gain, much leisure, and a great deal of recreation. Those who hold this view even believe that labor is unavoidable drudgery.
>
> However, labor holds a supreme value and profound meaning for man. Labor is effective in the overcoming of desire, tempering the will, and molding the personality. It is not just for existence or warmth and food; it refines the character.
>
> To summon up every fiber of one's being, to devote heart and mind to the unwavering performance of daily tasks is the most honorable form of self-cultivation. It can steel the soul and raise and improve thinking.
>
> There is a Latin proverb: 'The character of the worker is more important than the completion of the work.' However, the character of the worker can only be improved and perfected by working. A

proper philosophy of life can only be born through the sweat of labor and man's spirit can only be tempered through unremitting daily labor.

Those known in the world as 'celebrities,' people who have achieved the pinnacle of success in their own fields, must all have undergone a similar experience. Not only does labor create economic success, it also increases the value of man himself.

There is no need to break away from the mundane world, one's place of work is the best place in which to temper the will, work itself is the best form of self-cultivation, and conscientious work every day can mold nobility of character and lead to a life of happiness."

For the Protestant Christian church work was a sacred vocation, the underlying reasoning being that any calling was spiritual, a task ordained by God, and the seat of man's aims, mission, and values.

The German sociologist Max Weber (1864–1920), one of the most influential thinkers of the 20th century, made a profound study of the causal relationship between the Protestant ethic and the spirit of capitalism. He discovered that the core doctrine of all Protestant denominations was a "vocation from God" in which "the only way of living acceptably to God was not to surpass worldly morality in monastic asceticism, but solely through the fulfilment of the obligations imposed upon the individual by his position in the world. That was his calling." That is to say, the Protestant doctrine "rejected the ethical commandments of Roman Catholicism," thereby "investing secular conduct with a religious significance."

Weber's conclusions demonstrate that it was this sort of Protestant belief in vocation and the qualities of hard work, frugality, honesty, and integrity it bestowed on its adherents, that provided the strong ethical and driving force for the development of modern Western capitalism.

American historical figures such as Benjamin Franklin (1706–1790) and Nelson Rockefeller (1839–1937) were classic Protestants. Their ability to achieve such great success derived firstly from superior moral character and then because their Protestant ethic gave them the conviction that one should believe in one's calling as one believed in God and that one should love work as much as life.

In fact, taking a step back, you could say that as long as you use your abilities in an honest job to support your family then you have already fulfilled your role. For the Confucians, "fulfilling one's role" was an achievement in upright behavior. The achievement may have been very ordinary but it represented something worthwhile. In this sense, therefore, it was actually self-cultivation.

This apart, if you are a full-time wife without outside employment it might, at first sight, seem as if you were not creating value for society, but you only have to quietly concentrate on supporting your husband and raising your children and you will be fulfilling your role. At the same time, it is possible to achieve value in life through ordinary domestic work; this is also self-cultivation.

Chapter 8
Constructing an Innermost Being Impervious to Both Adoration and Insult

*A student asked Master Yangming:"Shusun Wushu slandered
Confucius, how may a sage be spared from defamation?"*

*Master Yangming said:"Slander comes from without. How may
even a sage avoid it? As long as man values self-cultivation and is
a sage through and through, even if he is slandered it cannot touch
him. If clouds obscure the sun how can they damage its light? If
one was a whited sepulcher, outwardly virtuous but evil within,
all would be revealed in the end even if nobody spoke of it. Hence
Mengzi said: 'There is inevitable slander but also unforeseen praise.'
Slander and praise both come from without, how may one avoid
them? Only through attention to self-cultivation."*

The story surrounding this student's question is contained
in the *Zi Zhang* chapter of the *Analects*. Shusun Wushu
was an official of the state of Lu who, for some reason,
regarded Confucius with disfavor and once remarked to
a fellow courtier: "Zigong is a great deal better than his
master Confucius." This remark was relayed to Zigong
who was instantly angered and said: "My master's virtue
far exceeds mine. To take the wall surrounding a house as
an example, the wall surrounding my house is only as high
as my shoulders and any passer-by can see the house and
consequently praise it for its elegance; the wall round my
master's house, though, is several tens of feet high and it
is difficult to get in, thus there is no way of knowing how

splendid and magnificent it is."

Not long after, Shusun Wushu once more slandered Confucius in front of others. This time, Zigong was truly furious and said: "Don't do this again, Confucius is beyond slander! The virtue of others may be reckoned as a mountain that may yet still be surmounted, but the virtue of Confucius is like the sun and moon and is insurmountable. Even if people want to sacrifice themselves to the sun and moon, what harm could come to the sun and moon themselves? It merely demonstrates how they have over-estimated their abilities."

Because of the existence of the record of this incident in the *Analects*, a thousand years later one of Wang Yangming's pupils was able to come to the aid of Confucius but he profoundly misunderstood the incident.

However, Wang Yangming's answer reflects something that he himself felt and had experienced.

Following Wang Yangming's suppression of the rebellion of the Prince of Ning in 1519, he was besieged by rumors and attacked from all sides, particularly by some of the duplicitous and obsequious ministers that surrounded Emperor Wuzong who, jealous of Wang Yangming's achievement, claimed that he had "conspired with the Prince of Ning" and that his motivation for putting down the rebellion was to kill people in order to silence voices.

At a time when Wang Yangming was besieged by vilification and slander, his ordinary practice of self-cultivation took on a greater role. Because of the fact that in his youth he had already mastered the art of

imperturbability and because of the experiences of exile
and enlightenment at Longchang, he had forged a strong
independent inner spirit impervious to both good and bad.
Thus, the stratagems of scheming courtiers, rather like the
clouds that obscured the sun, could not harm him.

During this time, Wang Yangming did what he had to
do, and studied what he needed to study while consistently
maintaining an acutely perceptive conscience and passing
the days in relaxed calm as usual. In his own words:
"One can only carry on according to conscience and with
endurance, regardless of sniggering slander and careless of
reputation" and "Inner strength will increase naturally and
the outer world will not interfere." (*Instructions for Practical
Living, Vol. III*)

One of Wang Yangming's pupils once asked him: "How
should a practitioner of the School of Mind regard anger?"

Wang Yangming's reply was: "How could one not be
angry?" Anger was difficult to avoid and the crux of the
matter was a grasp of a number of principles: first, not to
be angered more than was appropriate; next, to "take things
as they come" and "pay not a bit of attention." Finally, Wang
Yangming gave an example. If one saw people fighting on
the street, one would definitely feel indignation at the one
in the wrong; but although indignant, one should also be
"broad-minded and never betray the slightest anger." This
was knowledge of anger.

In sum, Wang Yangming made three points:

•Learn self-control when angered, keep within

appropriate limits, never go too far.

•Never hang on to anger, let it pass with the incident, do not harbor hatred.

•When angry, learn to transcend one's own views and find an objective third-party point of view. This is the only way to introduce reason into the situation and maintain broad-mindedness and a calm and untroubled atmosphere.

The best of the skills for enduring disgrace and humiliation is to regard the slanders, contempt, suffering, setbacks, adversity, and trials of life as a form of assistance like an indispensable whetstone upon which virtue, will, ability, and the perfection of character may be honed.

In Buddhist terms, this form of assistance is known as "accumulate the contrary and move upwards." That is to say that the negative factors in life may be considered essential conditions for the creation of true ability. In the words of Wang Yangming, "With true effort, man may derive benefit from slander and falsehood and make them a resource for the advancement of virtue." (*Instructions for Practical Living, Vol. III*)

A master of Tantric Buddhism was once preaching the Buddhist Law throughout Tibet and was accompanied by his chef. Not only did the chef lack culinary skills and a sense of responsibility, but he was also violent by nature and always getting into rows.

The local people observed the dreadful character of the chef and said privately to the master: "Master, why do you put up with the ill temper of your chef? He can only damage you and is of no help at all, why do you not send him on his way? We would be delighted to help you find another."

The master smiled and said: "You don't understand, I don't look on him as my servant but as my master."

The locals were astonished and said: "Master, why do you say that?"

The master said: "Every day his innate incompetence and aggressive nature teach me how to endure and how to cultivate patience. Consequently, I consider him extremely valuable and a teacher to me."

Obviously, the master made his chef an indispensable "accumulation of the contrary" on the road of self-cultivation. If we can learn from this master, what is there that we could not abide?

Chapter 9
Transcending Suffering

Lu Cheng was staying at the Honglu Monastery when he suddenly received a letter from home saying that his son was seriously ill. Lu Cheng was much troubled and could not bear it.

The master said:"This moment is propitious for hard work. If you let it slip what will be the use of learning in normal times. People should temper themselves in this kind of moment."

Instructions for Practical Living,Vol. I, Record of Lu Cheng

It is impossible to avoid all the suffering and adverse circumstances of life. We have two choices: we can meet them in a spirit of resistance and negativism and suffer greatly and possibly collapse in the process; or we can accept them calmly and positively, telling ourselves that since they are inevitable, it is best to face them with courage and a kind of respect.

Wang Yangming instructs us in the second choice, that is, no matter under what circumstances we should always maintain our inner freedom and use our spiritual strength to transcend all external situations.

In order to better understand the terms "inner freedom" and "spiritual strength" it is worth looking at a story from World War II.

The hero of the story is the eminent Austrian neurologist and psychiatrist Viktor Frankl who, following the German occupation of Austria, was imprisoned by the Nazis in the notorious Auschwitz concentration camp with his family because he was Jewish. He lost almost all his relatives in the camp. His father, mother, brother, and wife either died of suffering or directly in the gas chamber and crematorium. Everything in his life had been completely destroyed. Everything of value had been wrecked. He experienced hunger, cold, sickness, and beatings and there was not a moment of any day when he was not under the threat of death. Nevertheless, in the midst of the despair of fatal suffering and hopelessness, Frankl stubbornly continued to live out the meaning of life while maintaining his human dignity.

While his fellow sufferers were plunged into fear, paralysis, and despair, Frankl relied on his psychological background and achievements and the strength of his

inner mind to discover the meaning of suffering in life—
rather like finding a green shoot in permafrost. Frankl
believed that no matter what the circumstances, even in
the most dreadful of situations, a man still possessed a
kind of indestructible spiritual freedom, which he called
"the final inner freedom."When you cannot alter external
suffering you may still choose the way in which you face it
and accept it—you can live on like a living corpse, broken
in will and suffering, and quietly slip away into death one
night like an insignificant ant; or, even in the most difficult
circumstances, you can "uphold courage, self-respect
and selflessness" and always maintain love, humor, and
appreciation of art and nature to enable the strength of the
inner mind to transcend external fate; even if one must
die one should know how to do so "with pride and not in
miserable suffering."

In his later biography, *Man's Search for Meaning*, Frankl
gave a number of examples in order to demonstrate that
"suffering with dignity" was entirely possible. In the midst
of "that senseless world of despair" he would deliberately
concentrate on remembering and thinking about his wife
so that he could continue to live on in love; he would
"force" his fellow sufferers to tell jokes so as to "transcend
and distance their predicament" through a sense of humor.
Another example tells how one evening after a day of hard
labor, he and his fellows were resting exhausted on the
ground when one of them suddenly shouted to them to
go to the parade ground to watch the sunset. Frankl and
his friends then watched one of the most beautiful sights

on earth: the setting sun shining on the towering trees of the forest and the heavens filled with rust red and blood red clouds, the desolate grey brick huts standing silently amongst pools of muddy water that reflected the gleaming sky. After several minutes of stillness, one said to another: "How beautiful the world is!"

Frankl wrote: "As the inner life of the prisoner tended to become more intense, he also experienced the beauty of art and nature as never before. Under their influence he sometimes even forgot his own frightful circumstances." Writing of death, Frankl borrowed from the experience of another prisoner to express his own attitude to death. He said that this prisoner had made a contract with heaven when he arrived in the concentration camp. The contract stipulated that in exchange for his life, God would release from suffering all those whom he loved. It was not important whether or not they were his father and mother, his wife and children, or just some others. What was important was that through this kind of inner promise and resilience there would be some meaning to his suffering, his sacrifice would be worthwhile, and his death would not be "utterly senseless."

It was with this dignity that Frankl accepted the suffering of three years in a concentration camp. He believed that this was "a real inner achievement" since it not only demonstrated individual character but the nobility and dignity of human nature as well. After the war, Frankl put his unparalleled experiences and profound thought to good use as the basis for the creation of "logotherapy," a

means of helping people to discover the meaning of life and
to transcend its inevitable suffering. Frankl thus became
a successor to Freud and Adler and founder of the Third
Vienna School of Psychotherapy, achieving considerable
fame and influence.

Frankl's story teaches us that whatever the
circumstances, man should never become the plaything of
his environment but should, through proper means, live a
life of dignity and retain his inner freedom—the freedom
to make his own choices. In this way, there will be no
concentration camp that can confine you, or any fate that
can control you, least of all will there be any power that can
defeat you.

As far as Lu Cheng is concerned, the dangerous illness of his
son was, admittedly, a serious blow but seen from the point
of view of self-cultivation, it may have been an opportunity
to temper the will or to forge a strong inner mind, which is
why Wang Yangming told him: "This moment is propitious
for hard work."

There is a well-known Zen saying, "suffering is
enlightenment," meaning that suffering is an indispensable
condition of enlightenment: without it, there is no
possibility of enlightenment. His son's illness caused
Lu Cheng immense suffering in the same way that exile
to Longchang caused Wang Yangming great suffering.
Nevertheless, this is precisely the road to enlightenment.

On this basis we could say that a model with a positive
quality cannot be separated from its negative aspects or

mood. In other words, it is exactly because of the existence of negative aspects and mood that a positive model becomes possible. As Khalil Gibran said: "A pearl is a temple built by pain around a grain of sand."

As far as self-cultivation is concerned, neither external suffering nor internal pain are our enemies: they are the indispensable refiner's fire along the road of self-cultivation. It is precisely their existence that has created the conditions for the perfection of character and given us the possibility of changing and improving our nature. They also allow us greater possibilities to achieve successes difficult to reach under normal circumstances.

Like the unavoidable setbacks and suffering of living, the world in which we exist is also full of all manner of regrets, but it is only because of these regrets that we embark on the pursuit of perfection. Despite the fact that perfection can never be realized, it is in its untiring pursuit and approach that the soul is tempered, our character improved, and our nature can escape from disaster, baseness, and corruption to freedom, nobility, and purity.

Part IV

Exercise Conscience: Investigate for Knowledge, Act with Virtue and Eradicate Evil

All the learning of the sages is rooted in the elimination of the obstacles presented by selfish desires and in the recognition of the innate conscience of the inner mind. The entire practice of morality is nothing less than the fulfilment of the task of acting with virtue, eradicating evil from the mind, implementing morality in every aspect of life, and extending it to each and every matter or object.

Man is a combination of the spiritual and the animal. The more man is able to overcome the animal within him, the further behind he leaves the animal state and the closer he approaches the spiritual. Wang Yangming teaches us to "investigate for knowledge, act with virtue, and eradicate evil." This is the act of turning our backs on our animal characteristics and facing towards the spiritual. Once we have achieved this, it is as if our ordinary, trivial life has been blessed with a spiritual significance. This being so, we can say that the sacred realm of the sages is not a place but a path. In other words, man may never be able to become a god, but there is no limit set upon his approach to sagehood. Thus, within this unconfined approach, a life with value and with significance opens before us.

Chapter 10
Characteristics of the Four Great Values
of Conscience

The exercise of conscience is the engine of sage-like learning. It is the truth with which the sages seek to improve us.

Instructions for Practical Living, Vol. II, Reply to Ouyang Chongyi

The "exercise of conscience" is the crystallization of Wang Yangming's lifetime of study and wisdom. This proposition incorporates another two of his important propositions, "Mind is Principle" and "the unity of knowledge and action," so that it absorbs the complete sense of Wang Yangming's School of Mind and even the spirit of the doctrines of Confucianism. It allows the scholar to glimpse a single spot and yet see the whole leopard, "to understand all from a single word" and "have firm ground upon which to tread." (*Instructions for Practical Living, Vol. II*)

In the context of Wang Yangming's School of Mind there are two levels of meaning to the term "conscience": first, an awareness and sense of morality; second, the existence within man of a universal principle that transcends all sentient beings.

It can be seen from this that conscience is both integral to life and possessed by all. Nevertheless, for the generality of people, conscience is submerged and invisible, so that the sense and awareness of a preexisting morality is very easily lost in the life led later.

There is a tale told of one of Wang Yangming's disciples

who one night caught a burglar and, seeking to put into practice what he had learned, lectured him on the principles of conscience. To his surprise, the burglar burst out laughing and said: "Well, tell me, where is my conscience?"

The disciple was momentarily lost for words. It was a very hot day and seeing that the burglar was heavily clothed, he said: "It's too hot, why don't you take your jacket off?"

The burglar did as he was told.

The disciple looked at him and went on: "It's still too hot, why don't you take your trousers off as well?"

The burglar hesitated and said: "Maybe ... that's not quite right?"

The disciple yelled: "There, *that's* your conscience!"

"A sense of shame" is a sense and awareness of morality that no animal possesses but is unique to man. The fact that the burglar had a sense of shame is evidence that his conscience had not disappeared. It had merely been obscured by his evil and erroneous desires. This is what Wang Yangming termed "the obstacles presented by selfish desires." As he saw it, conscience resembled a bright mirror "as lustrous as a gem" and selfish desire was like the dust that "left unswept for a day acquires another layer." Thus, although conscience is a concomitant of everybody's life, it cannot appear in our lives of its own accord. If you wish conscience to appear and, like the bright mirror, illuminate all sentient beings, then effort must be devoted to "exercise."

"Exercise" combines three meanings: realize, expand, and implement. Realization is the discovery of our inner conscience; expansion is the perfection of our character and the strengthening of our moral ability; implementation is the practice of conscience in our daily lives.

It is not difficult to discover the fundamental spirit of Wang Yangming's School of Mind from the phrase "exercise conscience": all the learning of the sages is rooted in the elimination of the obstacles presented by selfish desires and in the recognition of the innate conscience of the inner mind; the entire practice of morality is nothing less than the fulfilment of the task of acting with virtue, eradicating evil from the mind, implementing morality in every aspect of life, and extending it to each and every matter or object.

In the context of Confucianism and of Wang Yangming's School of Mind, "conscience" has the four classic characteristics of spontaneity, self-sufficiency, self-discipline, and self-attainment.

Conscience is spontaneous, it responds to the summons and orders of the inner mind, not to the standards and demands of the outer world.

Conscience is self-sufficient, it gains nothing from external understanding, approval, or praise, nor does it lose anything through external misunderstanding, slander, or negative criticism.

Conscience is self-disciplined, it establishes its own rules and abides by them, it requires no outside encouragement or supervision nor does it give in to outside coercion or temptation.

Conscience is self-attained, its enjoyment is spiritual, its gain is the perfection of character, it is there in the moment, it does not hope for a future return; its aim is in itself and requires no other reward.

These four characteristic values of conscience are much the same as Kant's "Moral Law."

In Kant's view, the moral law is an instruction issued by man's rational sense to himself, an instruction about what he "ought" to do. However, there are two kinds of instruction, the "hypothetical imperative" and the "categorical imperative." It is only the latter that is genuine moral law.

The hypothetical imperative is conditional. For example, you rescue a drowning child and you think "If I perform this good deed, I will be known as a good person or I may be rewarded by the child's parents." In this case, your motive falls under the hypothetical imperative since your rescue was conditional and your aim was to gain reward. This cannot be regarded as a moral act.

The categorical imperative is unconditional—if you rescue the drowning child and act solely out of compassion and have no other motive at all than "I ought to help," then your motive falls under the categorical imperative, your means and aim are one and thus your act has moral value.

One can see from this that Wang Yangming's "conscience" also belongs to the classic categorical imperative because of its spontaneity, self-sufficiency, self-discipline, and self-attainment. It is a unity of means and aim and completely unconditional. Acting upon this inner moral command may not bring us any actual advantage but it invests our personal conduct with a value and dignity that is reflected in a freedom that belongs particularly to man.

As Kant saw it, man was both "a naturally existing phenomenon" and a "rational being." In the first sense, he was like any other animal, subject to all kinds of natural laws; in the second sense, man transcends the animal and acts in accord with the laws of reason.

The first is the territory of necessity, a physical world of the senses, while the second is the realm of freedom, a formless world of super-perception. Man lives simultaneously in both worlds. Although both worlds are intimately connected with the existence of self, they are utterly different in their relationship with the significance of the life of man.

Kant believed that as far as the physical world of senses was concerned, we are a part of nature and, like all other naturally existing phenomena, just a link in nature's endless chain of cause and effect. In the vast and limitless universe, our home—the earth—is just a speck in the ocean, an insignificant grain of sand, whilst we ourselves are minute organisms that live on it. We do not know upon what basis we have been granted this extremely brief life, nor do we know where and when we shall give it up and re-enter nature's eternal material cycle.

Viewed in this sense, mankind is just a limited, naturally existing phenomenon. Even if it possesses cognitive ability and is aware of the laws of nature and even if these laws of nature are bestowed upon nature through mankind's powers of understanding, it is of no help since, despite everything, it remains a naturally existing phenomenon, its status no different from that of a rock or a tree.

However, where the formless rational world is concerned things are different. This formless world of super-perception indicates to us that man is not just a naturally existing phenomenon but a rational being that, as a member of the world of reason, may endlessly improve the status and value of his character and intellect. In character, the self-discipline of the moral law produces a way of existence that is unique in animal nature and even unique in the sensory world as a whole, demonstrating that man, as a rational being, has the freedom to make his own rules and the true freedom to determine his own existence.

When acting according to the moral law he frees himself from the heteronomous status of being a mere "object" and achieves a freedom and dignity that transcends all naturally existing phenomena and is not confined by the limitations of nature.

All the above is a summary of Kant's own personal philosophy contained in the final part of *The Critique of Practical Reason*. In a certain sense, Kant's "Reason," "Intellect," and "Moral Law" could almost be equated with Wang Yangming's "Heavenly Principle" and "Conscience."

This is because they are the key to separating man from animals and the pillar that supports man's ability to transcend the animal state and the limitations of nature to achieve freedom and become the master of his own fate. Thus, we can say that the characteristics of the four great values of conscience, "spontaneity, self-sufficiency, self-discipline, and self-attainment," together with Kant's "categorical imperative," are the guarantee and conditions for man's realization of the ideal of freedom. They are also the only road from the realm of necessity to the realm of freedom open to man.

Chapter 11
The Journey Towards Self-Cultivation

The "investigation and correction of phenomena" is the investigation and correction of the phenomena of the mind, and the investigation and correction of the phenomena of meaning and of knowledge. (That is to say, the revision of erroneous states of mind, the revision of erroneous concepts, and the revision of erroneous perceptions.)

Instructions for Practical Living, Vol. II, Reply to Vice-Minister of Personnel Luo Zheng'an

The difficulties all lie in the investigation and correction of the acquisition of knowledge. This is precisely a matter of sincerity. Once ideas are sincere then the mind will in the main be correct of itself and self-cultivation will occur of itself.

Instructions for Practical Living, Vol. I, Record of Xu Ai

The Confucian system of self-cultivation involved a step-by-step method and procedure known as the "eight clauses": investigation, acquisition of knowledge, sincerity, rectification of the mind, self-cultivation, management of the family, government of the nation, peace under heaven.

There is a contextual trajectory that starts at "investigation" and ends at "peace under heaven," running from shallow to deep, from near to far, from self to others, and from small to large. The starting point of self-cultivation is also "investigation." Without "investigation" everything that follows is so much wasted space.

The Cheng-Zhu School of Reason believed that Principle lay at the heart of all things and of all sentient beings, so that "investigation" meant a thorough examination of the Principle within all things and sentient beings, the so-called "investigation of things to seek the Principle." However, when he was young and still accepted the views of the Cheng-Zhu School of Reason, Wang Yangming had spent seven days and nights conducting an "investigation" of a grove of bamboos, the end result being that it was effort wasted. Subsequently, it was only following his enlightenment at Longchang that he realized that "Mind is Principle."

Since Principle lay not in things but in the mind, it followed that there was no way that "investigation" could be conducted externally and that effort should therefore be devoted to the mind. Consequently, Wang Yangming's explanation of "investigation" was: "investigation is rectification, the rectification of that which is not rectified to return it to righteousness" (Wang Yangming, *An Enquiry into the "Great Learning"*).

Put simply, Wang Yangming's "investigation and correction of phenomena" is, in fact, the "investigation and correction of the phenomena of the mind" that is the correction of all the various erroneous and unhealthy desires, moods, concepts, attitudes, and viewpoints within the mind.

In other words, investigation is the establishment of virtue and the eradication of evil. In general, however, people are never particularly competent when undertaking the processes of investigation and the acquisition of knowledge. They clearly recognize what is virtuous, but out of considerations of profit and loss dare not uphold it; equally, they clearly recognize what is evil but because of the promptings of self-interest or out of habit they do it nevertheless.

This is self-deception, a lack of sincerity. Hence, in Wang Yangming's view, effective self-cultivation required time and effort to be spent on "sincerity." According to the classic Confucian text the *Great Learning*, sincerity was the absence of self-deception, a constant examination and reflection upon each of one's own thoughts, maintaining those that are virtuous and rejecting those that are bad. This was the only way to establish sincerity in reality.

In summary, it is not difficult to reach two conclusions:

(1) In the end, the topics of "investigation," "acquisition of knowledge," and "sincerity" in Wang Yangming's School of Mind all say one thing—establish virtue and eradicate evil.

(2) Sincerity is not a result that only appears after a long period of "investigation" and the "acquisition of knowledge." It should imbue the whole of these two processes from start to finish.

In point of fact, as far as Wang Yangming was concerned,

sincerity was not necessarily to be confined to the processes of investigation and the acquisition of knowledge, it could even be the very hub of the "eight clauses" and permeate the whole life of self-cultivation of Confucian scholars.

The reason that "sincerity" occupies a position of such unique importance in Wang Yangming's School of Mind lies in the fact that Wang Yangming's understanding of the term does not stop at the definition of "absence of self-deception." He combines it with its description in another Confucian classic, the *Doctrine of the Mean*, investing it with a meaning of broader scope and greater profundity.

There are numerous discussions of sincerity throughout the *Doctrine of the Mean*:

"Sincerity is the Way of Heaven; to act according to sincerity is the Way of man. With sincerity, those who achieve without striving, who gain without seeking, and serenely follow the Way of the Mean, these are sages; while those who act according to sincerity choose virtue and stubbornly maintain it."

"Sincerity is to become wholly perfect in oneself; and the Way is to lead oneself. Sincerity is the beginning and end of all things; if there is no sincerity, then there is nothing. This is why the ancients valued sincerity. Sincerity is not just the perfection of self; it is the perfection of all things. To perfect oneself is humanity (*Ren*); to perfect things is knowledge. The virtue of one's nature is a combination of the Way of both the internal and external worlds and hence appropriate for following at all times."

In the philosophical system of the *Doctrine of the Mean*, "sincerity" is the source of the universe and rather resembles the God of Christianity, Tathata of Buddhism, the Allah of Islam, the Dao of the Daoists, the Heavenly Principle of the School of Reason, and the conscience of Wang Yangming's School of Mind, in the way that they all occupy the summit of each system of thought.

Described in the language of today, sincerity (*cheng*) could be termed a universal law, a universal energy, an absolute spirit, the ultimate reality, and so on. It was precisely because of the profundity and expanse of the sublime position occupied by *cheng* in Confucian philosophy that in Wang Yangming's eyes "sincerity" was not just the "absence of self-deception." It would be better to say that the meaning of sincerity lies in the process of ridding oneself of evil and establishing virtue through investigation and the acquisition of knowledge in order to perfect one's character and form a secure connection between one's soul and the supreme entities of universal law, universal energy, absolute spirit, and ultimate reality. Moreover, to breathe as one with them and to be on the same wavelength.

Consequently, its practitioners have only to grasp sincerity, the hub of the practice of the School of Mind, and the effort put into investigation and the acquisition of knowledge and establishing virtue and eradicating evil will be successful. Thereafter, in time, as mind and body are rectified and cultivated, the aims of "management of the family, government of the nation, peace under heaven" become a natural possibility.

The "sincerity" upon which the Confucians and Wang Yangming placed so much emphasis was not just a means of self-cultivation, it also touched upon the motivation of self-cultivation.

Before we set out on the road of self-cultivation, we must all ask ourselves the question: "Why is it that I am doing this?"

If you are doing it for success and glory, then your self-cultivation is a betrayal of the principles of sincerity and problematic from the very start. Not only will it be ineffective but genuine success and glory may very well recede further and further into the distance.

However, if you are undertaking self-cultivation solely because you believe that the perfection of character is of fundamental benefit to you and for no other reason, then on the basis of this motivation, your character has already begun to improve and sooner or later success and glory may appear in your life.

When somebody acts only out of conscience and nothing else he is already "exercising conscience" and has released a powerful positive energy. This energy surges across the world and every place it reaches is transformed. At this point, there is no need to strive after success and glory since the things that people seek arrive unexpectedly. In other words, we should regard success and glory as by-products of the perfection of character; we should not use the perfection of character as a means of achieving success and glory.

To undertake self-cultivation for the purpose of

achieving a perfect moral character is a virtue in itself, or at least not far off a virtue.

To undertake self-cultivation in order to achieve success and glory is basically utilitarian and far removed from genuine self-cultivation.

Like Kant's "categorical imperative," genuine morality is unconditional: I want to be honest not because of the reputation for integrity or any other advantages that honesty may bring me, but because honesty is basically right and proper and worth upholding.

Thus, I am being honest for the sake of honesty alone and not for any other reason.

Mengzi's story of the child in the well is based upon the same principle: when we see a child about to fall down a well we immediately feel compassion; we rush to the rescue not because we want to make friends with the parents or to make a name in society but solely out of compassion.

Thus, I am rescuing somebody for the sake of rescue, not for any other reason.

In Wang Yangming's words this is called: "Sagehood is study for self, the importance is in the process and not the effect." (*Instructions for Practical Living, Vol. III*) The process is the process of self-cultivation itself; the effect is the consequences and results of self-cultivation. Genuine practitioners of Confucianism are only concerned with whether or not the process of self-cultivation is correct and whether or not it assists the process of self-perfection. They take no account of the consequences or results.

The sincerity (*cheng*) of the *Doctrine of the Mean* is a

sincerity that seeks self-perfection and achievement for no other reason; the sincerity (*chengyi*) of the *Great Learning* is one that seeks to establish a proper motive for self-cultivation and to avoid self-deception.

It is only by starting at this point, assisted by the techniques of acquiring knowledge through investigation and ridding oneself of evil and establishing virtue, that one can attain perfection of character and finally successfully achieve "government of the nation, peace under heaven."

Chapter 12
Realizing Spiritual Transcendence in the Mundane World

Lu Cheng asked about "reaching above."

The Master said: "In their teaching the later Confucians, coming across anything subtle or profound, would say that the 'reaching above' was not to be taught and would thereupon teach 'learning from below,' thus distinguishing the two. Learning from below is all that may be perceived by the eye, heard by the ear, spoken by the mouth, and thought by the mind; that which may not be perceived by the eye, heard by the ear, spoken by the mouth, or thought by the mind is 'reaching above.' For example, the cultivation and irrigation of trees is 'learning from below' but their growth day and night and the luxuriance of their stems and branches is 'reaching above.' How can man partake of their power? Hence, all that may be achieved through effort and described in language is 'learning from below' and 'reaching above' lies within 'learning from below.' Everything that the sages say, utterly profound as it is, derives from 'learning from below.' If the scholar devotes effort only to 'learning from below' he will achieve 'reaching above' naturally and need not seek it elsewhere."

Instructions for Practical Living,Vol. I, Record of Xu Ai

The terms "reaching above" and "learning from below" occur in the *XianWen* chapter of the *Analects*. The original text reads: "In my studies, I start from below and get through to what is up above" (*trans*. D. C. Lau), meaning that awareness and comprehension of the Heavenly Mandate and the Heavenly Way is achieved through the practice of self-cultivation and self-discipline in daily life.

The Heavenly Mandate and Heavenly Way of pre-Qin Confucian philosophy are largely identical to the Heavenly Principle of the Confucianism of the Song and Ming dynasties. In modern terms, they could be called a "Universal Principle" or "Ultimate Truth." However, irrespective of the term used, they share a common characteristic—they are abstract.

Although these abstract entities may have no apparent relationship with real life, they basically determine our quality of life. The answer to the question why is very simple. It is because man has a soul.

We nurture our body with food, our sensory organs with sight and sound, and our appetites and desires with money and power, but have you ever thought what it is that nourishes your soul?

Unless you believe that you do not have a soul, or

think that the soul plays no part in the happiness of man, you will need to find suitable sustenance to feed its hunger. Material success may satisfy our need to survive and our vanity and bring us joy and a sense of achievement but it will not deliver happiness, even less will it help us to find the meaning of life.

There are many successful people who are unhappy and many people whose material conditions are ordinary but who consider themselves happy. Have we ever thought why this should be so?

The answer is similarly simple—the former do not understand how to tend their soul whilst the latter know how to deliver the nutrients the soul requires.

The most important nutrients for the soul are the things of the spiritual world that seem remote from reality, the "abstract entities" that transcend the experiences of daily life.

If we wish to prevent our soul dying from nutritional deficiency then we must not just pursue "all that may be perceived by the eye, heard by the ear, spoken by the mouth, and thought by the mind." We must give equal attention to "that which may not be perceived by the eye, heard by the ear, spoken by the mouth, or thought by the mind."

Described in terms of philosophy, the former is the world of phenomena and experience and the latter the transcendental world of the noumenon. The former indicates a material existence and the latter a life of the spirit.

Wittgenstein, the well-known Austrian-British 20th-century philosopher (1889–1951), once said: "It is not how things are in the world that is mystical, but that it exists."

"How the world is" indicates the world of phenomena and experience and "all that may be perceived by the eye, heard by the ear, spoken by the mouth, and thought by the mind"; everything that belongs to our daily life, including science, falls within its scope. Attention to "that it exists" means the need to clarify how the world came about. Why does the world exist? These questions address the problems of the transcendental world of the noumenon and of the necessity of studying the entities in "that which may not be perceived by the eye, heard by the ear, spoken by the mouth, or thought by the mind." This is both a philosophical and religious proposition.

In Wittgenstein's context, "world" naturally includes everything that exists within it, so his statement might be put as follows: "It is not how things are in *life* that is mystical, but that it exists."

Science tells us that the world originated with the "big bang" and that man evolved from apes. This tells us how the world (life) came to exist. It does not tell us *why* life exists. For example, why was there a big bang? From what did the Singularity arise? If we are to believe the scientists, the universe after the big bang was a blind "primeval soup." How did it boil away to produce life? How did a single cell gradually become the ape and thereafter evolve into man with intelligence and a soul?

If you tell me that all this is totally random, then let us

look at the scientific data below. A physicist has calculated that under the most favorable conditions the protein molecules that constitute a cell require a total of 10^{242} years to form. Under ordinary natural conditions the length of time required is so long as to be beyond the imagination. In fact, however, living organisms appeared on earth after 1,000 million years, moreover, at a time when the earth was still a boiling globe of fire. That is to say that life appeared as soon as the earth started to cool. If one uses "random" as an explanation, then how does this randomness differ from meticulous design?

If you go for a walk in the desert and come across a rock, that is nothing strange, but if you find a watch would you think it was random? You would certainly believe that it was something designed and made by an intelligent life form.

What is interesting is that the harmonious order and level of precision of the universe look very much as if they were designed by a certain kind of will. In order to produce and maintain life, the earth requires an ingenious combination of innumerable conditions of innumerable aspects of astronomy, physics, heat, and chemistry. If the sun was a little larger or smaller, the angle of intersection between the planes of the earth's axis and its orbit would alter slightly, the amount and composition of the atmosphere and water would not be the same as it now, there would be no planets nearby such as Jupiter to attract comet strikes, and there would be no possibility at all of life on earth and even less of the emergence of mankind.

Many scientists, including Newton and Einstein,

confronted by such a wonderful, harmonious and perfect universe, and beyond awe and wonder, were unwilling to believe in the random and preferred to believe that it was all the creation of God. Einstein said: "The individual feels the futility of human desires and aims and the sublimity and marvelous order that reveal themselves both in nature and in the world of thought. I cannot conceive of a genuine scientist without that profound faith."

Of course, the religious faith that Einstein describes does not refer to the worship of a particular spirit or to a personalized God, but to a belief that the universe and all sentient beings and the life within it derive from a sublime and sacred source. In other words, faced with the proposition "Why does the world (life) exist," genuine scientists would be filled with humility and reverence and frankly admit that this sort of question was way beyond the scope of their intellect.

Apart from the question "Why does the world (life) exist?", there are others such as "Why is man alive?" and "Whence life and whither death?" that are not susceptible to scientific explanation and should be transferred to the province of philosophy and religion. It is the philosophical and religious thought devoted to these core propositions and the behavior that flows from them that constitute man's spiritual and moral life.

People today have only been concerned with whether or not their physical body fares well in this mundane world of dust. They show little concern for life itself, the origins of the universe, or the relationship between life and spirit.

We have, all along, had our eye firmly fixed on the worlds of phenomena and experience and severed our spiritual connection with the noumenal and transcendent worlds. This is one of the major causes of the inability of modern man to find a meaning in life and also of its ever-increasing emptiness and anxiety.

It is well known that the Confucians, a substantial component of Chinese culture, placed great emphasis upon the ethics and morality of everyday life. Even if their spiritual aim was "the unity of man with heaven" and "all sentient beings of heaven and earth as one body," it was an improvement and transcendence of human nature rooted in the world as it is. The path to the practice of self-cultivation too, always followed the direction of the practice of morality in everyday life. The maxim from the Confucian *Analects*: "… learning from below and reaching above" is the simplest and most concise summary of this characteristic thought. In the vocabulary of the *Doctrine of the Mean* it is expressed as "reaching the sublime but following the Way of the Mean"—whilst the way of the sages may be sublime, in practice it cannot depart from the day-to-day relationships of the mundane world.

In terms of world religion, this attribute of Confucianism most closely approaches the characteristics of humanism. If the Western belief in "denying the world to seek paradise" could be termed "external transcendence," then the tendency to value "the realization of spiritual transcendence in daily life" in Chinese culture might be termed "internal transcendence." However, irrespective of the method or means employed, the realization of the transcendence of the mundane world through spiritual purification and the improvement of human nature remains a common aspiration for both Eastern and Western cultures.

The Confucian tendency towards "internal transcendence" molded the fundamental character of Chinese culture as well as forming the spiritual foundations that supported the lifetime aspirations of countless Chinese people for thousands of years. From Confucius, through Mengzi, and up to Zhu Xi and Wang Yangming, the core spirit that runs through several thousand years of Confucian culture is the cultivation of body and mind on the basis of "achieving sagehood without departing the daily life of the people."

Zhu Xi wrote in a poem:

> "I saw the light and shade of sun and cloud
> Play across the path-side pool
> And asked: 'How so clear?'
> 'Because of fresh spring water,' it replied."

The pool represents your life and its actual state at the moment; the "fresh spring water" refers to your spiritual life and its connection to a higher spiritual noumenon. You must find this kind of "fresh spring water" before you can achieve purity and clarity in life or achieve a better quality of life.

Wang Yangming said: "Do not leave the day-to-day but build what was there before." The day-to-day refers to the daily life's requisites of food, clothing, shelter and work, oil, salt, soy sauce and vinegar. "What was there before" is what Zen calls the original self, the source of the world and of life. In the eyes of Wang Yangming and of the Zen school, one did not need to see through the "red dust" of life, or escape the mundane world, or deny mankind, or seek paradise, because genuine self-cultivation was spiritual improvement and transcendence and not physical escape or flight. It was the same as the reason for the beauty of the lotus not being because it had escaped mud but because it had grown in mud and yet had not been defiled. Thus, true self-cultivation should take place amid the daily life of oil, salt, soy sauce, and vinegar and should be perfected amongst the chaos and disturbances of the red dust. Once you achieved a transformation of one's nature through correct self-cultivation you would naturally discover that this world filled with filth and ugliness was in fact, and at the same time, the perfect Pure Land of Buddhism and the sacred paradise of purity.

Consequently, true "reaching above" is to be found in the midst of "learning from below." Life is not somewhere else; it is in the here and now.

Chapter 13
The Key to the World of the Mind:
The Four Rules of Conscience

In the year of 1527, Master Yangming resumed office and was ordered to put down rebellions in Si'en[1] and Tianzhou[2] As he was about to depart, his disciples Qian Dehong and Wang Ruzhong held a discussion on learning.

Wang Ruzhong raised the following teachings of the master as topics for discussion: "To be without virtue and without evil is the original state of the mind; to have both virtue and evil is an act of consciousness; to know virtue and evil is conscience; to behave with virtue and eradicate evil is the investigation of things."

Qian Dehong asked, "What is the meaning of all this?"

Wang Ruzhong replied: "I fear this is not the last word on the topic. If we say that the original state of mind is without virtue and without evil, then it follows that consciousness is without virtue and without evil and that conscience is conscience with neither virtue nor evil and that things too have neither virtue nor evil. If you say that consciousness has both virtue and evil, then the original state of mind must retain both virtue and evil."

Qian Dehong said: "The state of mind is of the nature of the Heaven and originally without virtue or evil, but people form habits of mind and the presence of virtue and evil appears in thought. It is through investigation, acquisition, sincerity, correction, and cultivation that we return to that original state. If, originally, there was neither virtue nor evil, there is nothing more to be said."

That night, sitting upon the Tianquan bridge, both sought correction from Wang Yangming.

Master Yangming said: "I am about to leave and wanted you

---

[1] Present-day North Wuming County in Guangxi Province.

[2] Present-day North Tianyang County, also in Guangxi Province.

both to come and talk through the meaning of this to a conclusion. The views of you both have their value and should not be held solely on the one side. The people I meet fall into two kinds: those who come to enlightenment easily, who achieve it from first principles and whose original state of mind was like a flawless diamond, who 'hit the target without shooting'; once enlightened, for these people, the noumenon is achieved and they perceive all, both internally and externally. The other, lesser kind have ingrained habits of mind, the noumenon is obscured and it is necessary to instruct them and instill the need 'to behave with virtue and eradicate evil' in their thinking; once this is achieved and the dregs have been totally eliminated the noumenon appears brightly. The views of you, Ruzhong, are those of the easily enlightened people of talent that I meet, and yours, Dehong, are those of the less enlightened for whom I establish rules. Each should take from the other to use and those in between, above and below, may be led upon the Way; if each maintains his own side, then people will be lost and many will never reach the Way."

He later said: "In future when you expound learning to friends do not forget my goals. 'To be without virtue and without evil is the original state of the mind; to have both virtue and evil is an act of consciousness; to know virtue and evil is conscience; to behave with virtue and eradicate evil is the investigation of things.' As long as you expound according to this argument of mine and in line with the individual situation of each, there should be little difficulty for this has always been an all-embracing skill. The highly talented are difficult to find. As to those who instantly and thoroughly understand the noumenon, even Cheng Hao and Confucius' disciple Yan Hui, did not dare assume an understanding of the Way. How can one lightly hope that others may do so? For those who have *formed habits of mind, it would be to encourage emptiness not to teach them to act with virtue and eradicate evil through the application of conscience and merely to think of the noumenon in a void. This is no minor failing and must be quickly demolished."*

On this day, both Wang Ruzhong and Qian Dehong became aware.

Instructions for Living, Vol. III, Record of Huang Xingzeng

The passage above represents the historically well-known "Tianquan Proof" of Song and Ming thought.

Wang Yangming was 56 when he was dispatched to Guizhou to put down the rebellions in Si'en and Tianzhou. The following year, having done so, he died on board when returning to his native village by boat. Seen in this light, the discussion that took place before he left for Guizhou acquires a particular significance. By coincidence, the subject of the discussion was the equally coincidental topic of the "Four Rules of Conscience." Consequently, the discussion can almost be regarded as the summation of Wang Yangming's lifetime of scholarship.

If the Tianquan Proof is Wang Yangming's own summation of his life of scholarship, then the Four Rules of Conscience are the ultimate code that unlock his spiritual world (and our own as well).

Taking a broader look at Wang Yangming's theories set out above, the first question worth examination is: why does he say that the noumenal mind of man is "without virtue and without evil"? The majority impression of the Confucian sages, especially Confucius and Mengzi, is that they always emphasized "the nature of man is by origin virtuous." Why is it that the view of human nature held by Wang Yangming is so at odds with that of Confucius and Mengzi?

In point of fact, the propagation of the idea of original virtue in man's nature began with the Cheng-Zhu School of Reason. The formulation on the quality of human nature in the Confucian *Analects* was "Men are close to one another by nature. They diverge as a result of repeated practice" (*Analects, Yang Huo, trans.* D. C. Lau). Mengzi put it: "The virtue in human nature is like the downward flow of water: man cannot be without virtue, water cannot but flow downwards." (*Mengzi, Gao Zi Shang*)

If Confucius believed that human nature was basically virtuous then it should have been "the same as one another," thus, how could it be "close to one another"?

If Mengzi believed that human nature was basically virtuous why did he not say so directly and why use the tendency of water to "flow downwards" as a metaphor?

We can see from this that in the view of Confucius and Mengzi, man was not innately virtuous but merely had a *tendency* towards virtue.

In the reality of today, to say that human nature is basically virtuous is clearly rather difficult. If it were truly so then the world would long have a been a club for the virtuous. Why does the world still contain such shocking ugliness, darkness, and injustice? We can see that when the Cheng-Zhu School of Reason advocates the basic virtue of human nature it is something that "ought to be" and not something that is "actual." "Ought to be" is a concept, "actual" is a judgement. Conceptually, we can of course regard making the nature of man virtuous as a desirable aspiration, but as a judgement it would be inadvisable to place too high an estimate on human nature.

Consequently, Wang Yangming's judgement that human nature possessed neither virtue nor evil is a judgement of "actuality."

Of course, Wang Yangming's statement that human nature possesses neither virtue nor evil was not intended to cancel out virtue and evil, even less to mix the two up, but was because the qualities of virtue and evil in human nature are fundamentally incapable of definition. Put accurately, the investigation of whether or not human nature is virtuous or evil is a false premise.

During World War II, Hitler murdered six million Jews and the German businessman Schindler saved the lives of thousands of Jews solely through his own efforts. You can say that the former was evil and the latter virtuous, but you cannot say that the inherent nature of the first was evil and the latter virtuous because it is impossible to discuss virtue and evil outside the context of their actions. In other words, setting aside motive, behavior, and consequence to conduct a fruitless discussion about the virtue and evil of fundamental nature has absolutely no significance.

It was precisely because of this that Wang Yangming proposed his Four Rules of Conscience: although the mind was "without virtue and evil," conceptually, however, (including action and conduct driven by concept), it was definitely "both virtuous and evil," and hence required a conscience "aware of both virtue and evil" to supervise it and, even more, the skill and means to examine it on the basis of "to act with virtue and eradicate evil."

Perhaps people may ask: did not Wang Yangming say that conscience was innate in man, something that was known without having to learn? Moreover, conscience is definitely virtuous, hence, is not man's original nature also virtuous?

Absolutely, conscience is innate and known without learning but it is not virtuous of itself. It is a moral awareness that distinguishes between virtue and evil. This moral awareness may inculcate a tendency towards virtue but it does not endow us with a nature of pure virtue without evil, nor can it automatically make us a person of virtue. A knowledge of virtue does not mean that you will definitely act virtuously and eradicate evil. You may choose to behave virtuously or you may choose to do evil, this is a freedom that you have.

Anybody may feel sympathy for the case of Mengzi's "child in the well." This sympathy is conscience, your innate moral awareness. Nevertheless, in this example there is the same moral awareness and the same sympathy, but different people may make different choices—A may choose to rescue the child, B may choose to call the police, C may choose to look on, and D may choose not to look. In this case, there is complete freedom of choice.

In the end, the reason the Four Rules of Conscience are rooted in the "investigation of things," the reason the

Confucians stress self-cultivation, is because all mankind possesses free will and may make its own choice between virtue and evil—if man was innately virtuous or innately evil, what would be the point of discussing investigation and self-cultivation?

Hence, the greatest revelation of the Four Rules of Conscience is the relationship of free will to morality.

Free will is the ability to choose and control one's own conduct. If there is no free will there can be no morality to speak of. For example, the rule of the animal kingdom is that the weak are prey to the strong but we cannot use this to say that animals are immoral, since all animal behavior is instinctive and there is no free will. When a severely mentally ill person commits murder or arson, he cannot bear criminal or moral responsibility since he has no way of recognizing or controlling his own behavior: he has lost his free will.

For the same reason, if the nature of man was by origin virtuous and whatever you did and how you did it was right, basically there would be no need for choice. At what point then could you discuss the value of morality? Let us imagine for a moment a situation in which future scientific development installs some robots with a computer program that allows them to "act heroically in a just cause," and a robot sees the child from Mengzi's "child in the well" story and rescues it. Would we applaud it for its sense of morality? Clearly we wouldn't. Because the robot was controlled by a computer program and had no room for individual choice.

It can be seen that the value of morality lies in freedom

of choice.

The reason that man is superior to animals lies in moral awareness and free will. If someone with moral awareness and free will readily adheres to the law of the jungle and falls completely under the control of material desire and sensual enjoyment, how much difference is there between him and an animal?

It is only moral awareness that distinguishes man from animals and thereby equips himself with the qualifications to conduct himself properly. This kind of qualification cannot be stripped away by external power—but it can be stripped away by oneself. When somebody is clearly aware of virtue but acts without virtue or is clearly aware of evil but acts evilly, he is using free will to strip away the qualities and qualifications that allow him to conduct himself properly.

For this sort of person, free will and moral awareness exist in a state of mutual conflict and he suffers from tension, anxiety, and uneasiness. Conversely, it is only when people know virtue and practice it, know evil and eradicate it, that they can achieve harmony with themselves and experience ease, freedom, peace, and joy.

In this sense, someone who is able to know virtue and evil and to practice virtue and eradicate evil requires no reward from others: a clear conscience is already his greatest reward. However, for somebody who is clearly aware of virtue but lacks the strength to practice it and well knows the nature of evil but persists in doing it, there is no need to await punishment: he is already punishing himself. His greatest punishment is internal conflict and uneasiness.

Chapter 14
Establishing the Will to Achieve Sagehood

Lu Cheng asked about the "establishment of will."

Master Yangming said: "To think always of the existence of the Heavenly Principle, that is the establishment of will. If one never forgets this, then over time one's mind will naturally cohere in the way that Daoists achieve their immortal body. The continual existence of the Heavenly Principle will gradually lead to the states of Beauty, Greatness, Sagacity, and Divinity; this all grows and expands from the one idea."

Instructions for Practical Living, Vol. I, Record of Xu Ai

The qualities of "Beauty, Greatness, Sagacity, and Divinity" refer to four successive aspects of human character and were proposed by Mengzi who said: "The desirable is called 'good.' To have it in oneself is called 'true.' To possess it fully in oneself is called 'beautiful,' but to shine forth with this full possession is called 'great.' To be great and be transformed by this greatness is called 'sage'; to be sage and to transcend the understanding is called 'divine.'" (*trans.* D. C. Lau)

Wang Yangming tells us that even these states of Beauty, Greatness, Sagacity, and Divinity described by Mengzi started from the establishment of will.

The establishment of will is the starting point of Confucian study and self-cultivation and no teacher of self-cultivation, from the pre-Qin Mengzi and Confucius to Cheng Hao, Cheng Yi, Zhu Xi, Lu Jiuyuan and Wang

Yangming of the Song and Ming dynasties, ever began elsewhere. Confucius said, "When I was 15, I had the will to study." Mengzi said that in order to study one should "Make one's stand on what is of greater importance in the first instance" (*trans.* D. C. Lau), and Wang Yangming said "In study, for the most part, you may want a brain, but it's just the establishment of will" (*Instructions for Practical Living, Vol. II*).

However, the establishment of will propounded by Wang Yangming and the Confucians is utterly different from that understood by the generality of people.

When people generally speak of the establishment of will or determination, they usually mean the determination to achieve some future aspiration or vision, for example in career, position, or status, the earning of money or achievement and reputation and lifestyle. However, none of this is the establishment of will of the Confucians and Wang Yangming's School of Mind.

In Chinese, *zhi* (志), the character for "will," is a combination of *shi* (士) "scholar" on top with *xin* (心) "heart" or "mind" underneath, meaning the *xin* that a person possesses. This *xin* is not the physiological heart but refers to the mind, to character and to the whole spiritual world. It includes major concepts like world outlook, outlook on life, and values. It also includes ways of thought, conduct, and attitude, as well as character, emotion, temperament, ability, and habits. In a word, *xin* comprises the whole of a person's spiritual image, the sum of their inclinations, and their psychological characteristics in relation to stability.

Described in a single word it would be "personality." Consequently, true determination or establishment of will is not what you hope for in terms of career, status, or position, but what sort of personality you decide to be.

The Confucians mainly divided their concepts of personality into sages, worthies, gentlemen, and rogues.

The personality of the sage was one in which virtue was developed to the utmost and morality and wisdom reached their highest state. The worthy possessed a comparatively good moral character, knowledge, and ability. The gentleman was morally refined and spiritually different from the common run of people. The rogue was selfish, false, in pursuit of fame and profit, and with no sense of honor or shame nor of justice or humanity.

It is easy to see that for the Confucians and Wang Yangming the ideal personalities were those of the worthy and the gentleman, and the ultimate aim of study and self-cultivation was to be sage. Thus, when Wang Yangming calls upon people to "establish will" he means "establish the will of a sage" (*Instructions for Practical Learning, Vol. II*). The very kernel of establishing the will is to "continually preserve the Heavenly Principle."

In Wang Yangming's School of Mind, Heavenly Principle has the same meaning as conscience. Thus, continually preserving the Heavenly Principle really means continually exercising one's conscience.

"Preserving the Heavenly Principle, eradicating the desires of men" was the fundamental aim of the whole Song and

Ming dynasties School of Reason including Wang Yangming's School of Mind. However, since the beginning of the 20th century this proposition has been the subject of considerable criticism on the part of numerous commentators. Principal amongst the reasons has been a universal misunderstanding of the implied meaning of the phrase "the desires of men," which is taken as meaning the basic wants of man. In fact, the School of Reason in no way seeks to deny the logic for the existence of the desires of men. Zhu Xi, for example, believed that they had a fundamental existence and could not, indeed, ought not to be completely constrained. He said: "Although a sage cannot be completely without feeling" … "if it is a case of him being hungry and desiring to eat or thirsty and wishing to drink, then how can that desire be forgone?"

Confucius also said: "Eating, drinking, man and woman, these are the great desires that exist" referring to the physical needs of clothing, food, shelter, and behavior, "man and woman" meaning human sexual needs. These are all reasonable physical desires that should not be forbidden but should actually be afforded a certain degree of satisfaction. For example, Confucius once visited the state of Wei and after seeing the crowded conditions there, one of his disciples asked what was to be done in future, given that the population of Wei was already so large. Confucius replied: "Prosper them." The disciple went on to ask: "And when that is done?" Confucius replied, "Instruct them." It can be seen from this that Confucius advocated the satisfaction of their material desires before people were taught to seek perfection of character—the concept of "First prosper then instruct."

Since between Confucius and Zhu Xi there had never been a total denial of human desire, what is the meaning of "eradicating the desires of men" advocated by the School of Reason?

In fact, in this case "human desire" cannot simply be equated with the "desires of men," it refers to desire that exceeds reasonable bounds and offends proper principles.

Put simply, what the School of Reason wanted to destroy was the material desire that burst the dam of morality and recklessly flooded society rather than the normal desire that operated within the scope of morality and the law. In the words of Zhu Xi: "(Inappropriate) desire is like the flow of water that brings about a flood." The word "flood" here indicates something that exceeds reasonable bounds and offends proper principles. So far as general physiological and psychological needs are concerned, they are of course proper and at the same time moral.

Fundamentally, neither the School of Reason nor the School of Mind promote the banning of desire, nor do they approve of debauchery. They just teach continence.

Hence, when Wang Yangming and the School of Reason teach the preservation of the Heavenly Principle and the eradication of the desires of men, they are not demanding that people should abandon the seven emotions and six desires[1] but are asking that they should hold to a certain standard in everything they do and respect reasonable and proper principles. They should abide by the virtues of moderation to prevent a flood of emotion and a surge of desire, thus allowing us to stand firm amidst the red dust of the brimming material desire of the mundane world. We can be masters of ourselves, maintaining independence of character and a dwelling place for freedom of spirit and morality, without blind conformity, losing one's way, turning reality on its head, or dissimulation.

Man is an amalgam of the animal and the divine, a body that contains within itself both the Heavenly Principle and desire. The crux is not whether or not we can achieve the divine and wondrous state of character represented by "Beauty, Greatness, Sagacity, and Divinity" but whether we are willing to take the road to the divine. The more a man can overcome his animal instincts (eradicate human desire), the further he is removed from the animal state and the closer he approaches the divine (the maintenance of the Heavenly Principle). It is during this process that the improvement of human nature is realized.

As to this, in teaching us to "establish will" and "preserve the Heavenly Principle," Wang Yangming is asking and enabling us to turn our backs on our animal state and turn towards the divine. When the day comes that we are

---

[1] Translator's note: Generally speaking, the seven emotions refer to the expression or action within the mind of Joy, Anger, Anxiety, Grief, Thought, Fear, and Astonishment. The six desires are the physical desires or aspirations of the organs: Eye, Ear, Nose, Tongue, Body, and Sense.

in this position, it will be as if our normal humdrum, day-to-day existence has been endowed with a kind of divine significance. In this respect, we could say that the state of divinity is not a place, but a road. In other words, man can never become a god, but there are no limits upon him moving towards the divine. It is through this boundless approach that a life of value and meaning unfolds before us.